Heschel, Hasidism, and Halakha

HESCHEL,
HASIDISM,
and HALAKHA

Samuel H. Dresner

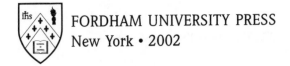

FORDHAM UNIVERSITY PRESS
New York • 2002

Library of Congress Cataloging-in-Publication Data

Dresner, Samuel H.
    Heschel, Hasidism and halakha / by Samuel H. Dresner.
        p.   cm.
    Includes bibliographical references and index.
    ISBN 0-8232-2115-6 (hardcover)—
    ISBN 0-8232-2116-4 (pbk.)
    1. Heschel, Abraham Joshua, 1907–1972.   2. Jewish
scholars—United States—Biography.   3. Heschel, Abraham
Joshua, 1907–1972—Views on Hasidism.   4. Hasidism.
5. Heschel, Abraham Joshua, 1907–1972—Views on Jewish
law.   6. Jewish law.   7. Judaism—Customs and practices.
I. Title.
BM755.H34 D74   2002
296.3′092—dc21   2001051077

CONTENTS

ACKNOWLEDGMENTS

I WOULD LIKE to express my gratitude to Dr. Edward K. Kaplan and Dr. Menachem Schmeltzer for their generous assistance with the final preparation of this manuscript for publication. They gave unselfishly of their time and professional expertise to complete details that my husband was unable to do before he died.

Dr. Fritz Rothschild and Rabbi Morton Leifman lent the encouragement I needed to bring this work to completion.

Dr. Elie Wiesel crowned this work with his words of approval as his expression of the abiding love and respect he has extended to my husband and to our entire family for many years.

These people acted in the truest spirit of friendship and collegiality. I thank them in the name of my husband (may his memory be a blessing), myself, and my children.

RUTH R. DRESNER

INTRODUCTION

SAMUEL H. DRESNER, whose spiritual legacy is embodied in this graceful and discerning book, became a lifelong disciple of Abraham Joshua Heschel in the fall of 1942. The bonding took place at the Hebrew Union College (HUC) in Cincinnati, Ohio, the rabbinical seminary of Reform Judaism. Heschel at age thirty-five was among several refugee scholars saved from the Nazis by HUC President Julian Morgenstern. Heschel arrived in the United States in 1940 fully prepared to bear witness to the living God of the Hebrew Bible. And Samuel Dresner was fully prepared to be inspired.

By 1942 Heschel already mastered literary English, speaking it with the accent of his mother tongue, the Yiddish idiom of his childhood and youth in Warsaw, Poland. During class Heschel made a remark that elicited a jolt of receptivity from Dresner. Quoting from Pirke Avot (Ethics of the Ancestors), Heschel asserted: "The shy person cannot learn and the impatient person cannot teach, so you don't be shy and I won't be angry." The American student recognized an authentic spiritual voice, bringing him closer to the holiness of Judaism. After many classes and conversations with Heschel, Dresner declared that "Heschel was the greatest Jew of his time. I wanted him to be my teacher."

And an effective, though gentle teacher he was. Samuel Dresner's voyage from assimilation through American Reform to the retrieval of traditional Judaism was exemplary. As a high school teenager, Dresner enjoyed a good time, sports, and girls. Then he experienced a dramatic insight. In downtown Chicago he encountered a destitute woman and realized he had never before thought about poverty. Appalled at his indifference, and encouraged by his rabbi, Felix Levy, an intellectual leader of Reform Judaism, young Sam sought answers to fundamental questions about evil, moral responsibility, and God.

He started at the beginning, studying Chumash (Torah) with Rashi's commentaries. At Northwestern University he majored in philosophy and decided to become a Reform rabbi—against his parents' admonition that he join an uncle's business. Instead he matriculated at the Hebrew Union College where he met Heschel, who became his model of Jewish learning, holiness, and social conscience.

In the 1940s, HUC still maintained the classical Reform ideology of previous decades—opposition to "supernaturalism," denial of authoritative Jewish law (halakha), the rejecting of such imperatives as kosher food and Sabbath restrictions—and the Reform prayer book was highly abridged, with worship services mostly in English. Heschel taught Sam the traditional daily morning prayers, using the tefillin (phylacteries) that belonged to his ancestor, the great Hasidic master Rabbi Levi Yitzhak of Berditchev.

Sam organized a group of sympathetic students. His devotees were called, somewhat humorously, the "Kavanah Boys." (Kavanah is the Hebrew term for "intention" or spiritual fervor associated with prayer and Hasidism.) They received satiric nicknames: Peter Levenson, a German rabbinical student from Berlin was "pious Pete," Robert Bergman was "mitzvah Bob," Albert Plotkin was "transcendental Al," and the zealous ringleader, "Kavanah Sam." The class's boldest intellectuals remained on the fringe, Richard Rubenstein, Eugene Borowitz, and Sam's childhood friend, Arnold Jacob Wolf, all of whom were touched by Heschel and became prominent in American Jewish life.

Sam Dresner deepened his commitment to tradition by following Heschel, in 1945, to the Jewish Theological Seminary in New York, the Conservative rabbinical academy. Dresner was ordained a Conservative rabbi and, under Heschel's direction, completed a doctoral dissertation on the ideal Hasidic leader; published with a preface by Heschel in 1960, *The Zaddik* became a classic. Rabbi Dresner became an eloquent and forceful pulpit preacher, a passionate scholar, and bold moral activist, serving Conservative congregations in Springfield, Massachusetts, and Chicago, Illinois.

Rabbi Dresner's many books flow from his calling to elevate the spiritual life of his congregants. Inspired by Heschel, he wrote essays and books to enhance Jewish practice, *The Sabbath, The Jewish Dietary Laws*, and the lovely meditative volume, *Prayer, Humility, and Compassion* (1957). He served the community on the Synagogue Council of America, the National Council of the Joint Welfare Board, the Rabbinical Assembly, and for ten years (1960–1970) as editor of *Conservative Judaism*. Like many liberal Jewish activists of the 1960s who defended civil rights for African Americans and denounced the implications of atomic warfare, Dresner became disillusioned in the 1970s and eventually turned toward the political right, redirecting his moral passion.

When he retired as a congregational rabbi, he and his wife, Ruth, a psychiatric social worker, returned to New York where he taught Hasidism and Jewish Philosophy at his alma mater, the Jewish Theological Seminary. Critical of developments in civil rights organizations, the women's movement, and Jewish Renewal, he devoted himself to saving accepted social norms. In 1994, already ill, he completed a gracious and loving book, *Rachel*, a retrieval of sacred sources relating to the Jewish woman. Reflecting his polemical side, Dresner's acerbic critique of popular culture, *Can Families Survive in Pagan America?*, appeared the following year.

All the while, aware that his time and energies were limited, Samuel Dresner brought to fruition his lifelong dream of publishing the life story of his teacher and master. Over the years he persistently collected an archive of documents, interviews, and insights that formed the foundation of the biography I had the honor to co-author with him, *Abraham Joshua Heschel, Prophetic Witness* (Yale University Press, 1998).

The present book reflects Rabbi Dresner's own special expertise on Hasidism and his loyal attachment (as critical as it might be) to the Conservative movement. In chapter one, he introduces readers to his remarkable teacher, celebrating Heschel's life and defining his guiding principles. With undisguised love, Dresner illustrates how a wide variety of people—Christians, Muslims, Jews, African Americans, and others—appreciated, and even revered, Heschel as a thinker, prophetic activist, and spiritual guide.

Chapter two, "Hasidism," includes Dresner's wide-ranging preface to Heschel's posthumous book, *The Circle of the Baal Shem Tov*, which he expertly edited. Few people are aware of Heschel's monographs on Hasidic masters, published in Hebrew or in Yiddish, and Dresner lucidly explains how Heschel, had he lived longer, might have absorbed these meticulous studies into a scholarly biography of the Baal Shem Tov, the founder of Hasidism.

It is indeed fascinating to ponder how Heschel remained faithful to his Hasidic soul, even after he earned a Ph.D. in philosophy from the University of Berlin. He was unique in that he combined the essence of Jewish piety—standing before the living God—with forthright responses to present-day challenges such as disbelief, virulent anti-Semitism, racism, interfaith dialogue and cooperation, the State of Israel, Soviet Jewry, peace, economic justice.

Dresner demonstrates how Heschel confronted the central issue of Jewish observance in his third and final chapter, "Halakha." Convinced that Judaism and the Jewish people will survive only if the authority of religious law is taken seriously, both Heschel and Dresner, in their different ways, support tradition while recognizing the frailty of today's spiritual seekers. After carefully surveying Heschel's views and writings on Jewish law, many of them previously unpublished, Dresner attempts to formulate a golden mean for contemporary Jewish practice.

That task is ours to continue. Rabbi Dresner guides us with his insights into "the tension of polarities" that characterizes Heschel's Judaism—a dynamic, unending adventure in the presence of God. It remains to be seen if his quest for a "vital center," with Abraham Joshua Heschel as a model, will help resolve today's Jewish civil wars. I, for one, would favor tolerance of differences as the first step, with reverence for divine image of all human beings as the practical goal.

The great virtue of Rabbi Dresner's book is to invite such dialogue.

We all benefit from Samuel Dresner's loving and learned conversation with his teacher, for they reach a fuller understanding in a "depth theology" beyond words, beyond ideologies. We are grateful that Rabbi Dresner clarifies the ideals they shared. "May their memory be for a blessing."

Brandeis University   EDWARD K. KAPLAN

1

Heschel

DYING WITH A "KISS" (DECEMBER 1972)

LET US BEGIN at the end.

Several years before Abraham Heschel's death in 1972, he suffered a near-fatal heart attack from which he never fully recovered. I traveled to his apartment in New York to see him. He had gotten out of bed for the first time to greet me and was sitting in the living room when I arrived, looking weak and pale. He spoke slowly and with some effort, almost in a whisper. I strained to hear his words.

"Sam," he said, "when I regained consciousness, my first feelings were not of despair or anger. I felt only gratitude to God for my life, for every moment I had lived. I was ready to depart. 'Take me, O Lord,' I thought, 'I have seen so many miracles in my lifetime.' "[1]

Exhausted by the effort, he paused for a moment, then added: "That is what I meant when I wrote [in the preface to his book of Yiddish poems]":

" 'I did not ask for success; I asked for wonder. And You gave it to me.' "

"Khob gebetn vunder anshtot glik, un du host zey mir gegebn."

Leaving Heschel's home, I walked alone, in silence, aimlessly, oblivious of others, depressed by the knowledge that the man who meant so much to so many was mortally ill.

I pondered his words. What had he meant by them? Was it possible to accept death so easily? Death. Faceless enemy, fearsome monster who devours our days, confounds the philosopher, silences the poet, and reduces the mighty to offer-

An earlier version of this chapter appeared in *Abraham Joshua Heschel: Exploring His Life and Thought*, ed. John C. Merkle (New York: Macmillan, c1985), pp. 3–27.

ing all their gold, in vain, for yet another hour! Was he telling me not to grieve overmuch, thinking of my feelings when he was moving toward the end of all feeling? Could he have been consoling me?

Suddenly there rang in my mind the striking passage with which he had concluded his first major work, *Man Is Not Alone*:

> Our greatest problem is not how to continue but how to return. "How can I repay unto the Lord all his bountiful dealings with me?" (Psalms 116:12). When life is an answer, death is a home-coming. . . .
>
> The deepest wisdom man can attain is to know that his destiny is to aid, to serve. . . . This is the meaning of death: the ultimate self-dedication to the divine. Death so understood will not be distorted by the craving for immortality, for this act of giving away is reciprocity on man's part for God's gift of life. For the pious man it is a privilege to die.[2]

And I found myself recalling a Hasidic teaching he often quoted. "There are three ascending levels of mourning: with tears—that is the lowest. With silence—that is higher. And with a song—that is the highest."

I understood then what it was I had experienced: the lesson that how a man meets death is a sign of how he has met life. Intimations of melody countered my sadness. At that moment the power of the human spirit, mortal and frail though it is, never seemed so strong.

Ten days before his death, Heschel had taped a television interview for NBC and was asked by the interviewer at the close of the program if he had a special message for young people. He nodded his head and seemed to turn to the future he would never see.

"Remember that there is meaning beyond absurdity.

"Know that every deed counts,

"That every word is power. . . .

"Above all, remember that you must build your life,

"As if it were a work of art. . . ."

The day before his death, Heschel insisted upon traveling

to Connecticut to stand outside a federal prison in the freez-
ing snow, waiting for the release of a friend, a priest, who
had been jailed for civil protest.

He died on the Sabbath eve, in his sleep, peacefully, with
a "kiss," as the ancient Rabbis describe the death of those
who die on the Sabbath. At his bedside were two books: one
a Hasidic classic, the other a work on the war in Vietnam.
The combination was symbolic. The two books represented
two different worlds: eternal spirit and mundane present,
mysticism and diplomacy, heaven and earth. Most choose
one over the other. Heschel refused to ignore either, preferring to live in the tension of polarity.

After the close of the Sabbath and before the funeral a
strange gathering of friends collected in his home to comfort
the family: there were several former students, a Hasidic
rabbi, an esteemed writer on the Holocaust, a well-known
Catholic priest, and Heschel's last disciple, the son of the
founder of a Japanese sect.

How to mourn? with tears, with silence, with a song?

HUMAN GRANDEUR AND DIGNITY

In a time of such madness that the earth threatens to explode
in our hands, how else to preserve sanity than by recalling
saints of old with whom to commune, by pouring over enlightened texts from which to regain insight, and, above all,
by identifying one who faced the absurd and the demonic
and yet triumphed: who dared speak, even sing, of the glory
of God and the marvel of man, of heavenly grace and human
compassion? In a period of divine eclipse, it is well to focus
on the life and work of someone upon whom Heaven's light
continued to shine.

In some ways it would be easier to treat Heschel the philosopher, the biblical scholar, or even the poet, for then an
area of investigation would be marked out and the printed
word available for all to examine. To discuss Heschel the
man, however, is another matter—perhaps a more difficult

matter. Not only his words, but also his dreams, his deeds, his entire life now become the subject of inquiry.

Inquiries such as this are fraught with danger, because ours is an age that flaunts irreverence, when debunking has taken on all the trappings of a national sport, and when historians revel in revealing the clay feet of the mightiest. Heschel himself once observed that "Suspect thy neighbor as thyself" had become the newly emended version of the commandment. Contemporary biographers, nurtured in this subversive view of humanity, tend to be skeptical of human dignity.

However, a major theme of Heschel's writings was human grandeur and dignity. For this, we find no argument more compelling than his works. As a youth, he titled his first book of poems *Der Shem Hameforash: Mentsh* (Man: The Ineffable Name of God). For our purpose, the question is not so much what he intended by his defense of human grandeur as how his views were related to his own life. "My father," his daughter has testified, "was the kind of man he wrote about."[3] Could he have written the following passage, for example, without experiencing something of what he wrote?

> Awareness of God is as close to him [the pious man] as the throbbing of his own heart, often deep and calm but at times overwhelming, intoxicating, setting the soul afire. The momentous reality of God stands there as peace, power and endless tranquility, as an inexhaustible source of help, as boundless compassion, as an open gate awaiting prayer. It sometimes happens that the life of a pious man becomes so involved in God that his heart overflows as though it were a cup in the hand of God.[4]

✳ MASTER STYLIST ✳

A master of English prose, though he knew little of that language when he arrived in America in 1940, Heschel, like his Hasidic forebears, had the gift of combining profundity with simplicity. He found just the right word not only to express what he thought but also to evoke what he felt, startling the mind and delighting the heart as well as addressing and challenging the whole person. So compelling are his sentences that a single paragraph often offers an embarrassment of riches. One reader, overwhelmed by this plenty, suggested studying Heschel like a page of the Talmud, that is, weighing with care each sentence, each phrase, each word. In contrast to the sustained thinking of Heschel's writings, and following the adage that less is more, the reader may at times want to stand still and dwell upon the kernel of a word, or a phrase, or a sentence, that he might better taste the whole loaf of Heschel's thought. There are passages in his writings that, once encountered, will be taken up again and again, until they are absorbed into one's inner life.

THE DIVINE IMAGE

"Emblazoned over the gates of the world in which we live is the escutcheon of the demons. The mark of Cain in the face of man has come to overshadow the likeness of God"—so Heschel wrote while still living in Hitler's Germany.[5]

The nineteenth century saw the shaking of the foundations of faith in God. We who dwell in the twentieth-first century have experienced the collapse of faith in the rival who was to replace Him: man. Poets applaud the absurd, novelists explore the decadent, and men prostrate themselves before the deities of lust and power. Our obsession is with human flesh. The ghoul who devours it is the latest film craze; the science of feeding it, firming it up, and preparing it for fornication is the most popular theme in literature. Daring to affirm common pieties such as marriage and children is to be subversive, while deconstruction obliterates all meaning but orgasm, which reigns supreme. Daily we are bombarded with lurid reports on the mass-killer, the rapist, and the corrupt bureaucrat. The fantasies of even little children are now peopled with perverts and the radiated dead.

Who will speak for those who do justice, love mercy, and walk humbly? At such a time we need nothing so much as to be reminded of the divine image in which we are framed, of our purpose on earth. I know of no writer who has done this more powerfully, eloquently, and convincingly than Rabbi Abraham Joshua Heschel.

He knew he was the descendent of a people who, ever since Sinai, was destined to "dwell apart" and whose vocation was to be a witness to the living God amidst all the idolatries of history. Because he was spared from the flames that devoured his family, his community, and the whole irreplaceable world of learning and piety of Eastern Europe, which alone could have produced him, Heschel felt a special burden had been placed upon his shoulders. He reminded us, with a testimony all the more convincing from one who had experienced consummate evil, that, despite the absurdity and the apathy, our world is marked by mystery and meaning, by wonder and joy; that we have the power to do God's will; and that the divine image in which we are framed can be distorted but not obliterated. In the end, he believed, the likeness of God will triumph over the mark of Cain.

SHALEM

Who was Rabbi Abraham Joshua Heschel? He was *shalem*, a person marvelously whole.

Environment

Consider the worlds of his *environment*.

Born in Warsaw, Poland, in 1907, a descendent of an illustrious line of Hasidic rabbis, Heschel, even from early childhood, was viewed with great expectations. When he was four or five, scholars would place him on a table and interrogate him for the surprising and amusing answers he would give.

When his father died during his ninth year, there were

those who wanted the young boy to succeed him almost at
once. He had already mastered many of the classical religious
texts; he had begun to write, and the words he spoke were
a strange combination of maturity and youth. The sheer joy
he felt as a child, so uncontainable at times that he would
burst out in laughter when meeting a good friend in the
street, was later tamed into an easy sense of humor that added
to his special personal charm.

Along with his talent for acquiring knowledge at an
astounding rate and his keen understanding was a growing
awareness that we dwell on the tangent of the infinite,
within the holy dimension, that the life of man is part of the
life of God. Some Hasidic leaders felt that in Heschel a renewal of their movement, which had grown dormant in the
twentieth century, might come about. Others, too, were
aware of the new light that was glowing in their midst.

Speaking about his early childhood, Heschel wrote:

> I was born in Warsaw, Poland, but my cradle stood in Mez-
> bizh (a small town in the province of Podolia, Ukraine),
> where the Baal Shem Tov, founder of the Hasidic movement,
> lived during the last twenty years of his life. That is where
> my father came from, and he continued to regard it as his
> home. . . .
> I was named after my grandfather, Reb Abraham Joshua
> Heschel—"the Apter Rav," and last great rebbe of Mezbizh.
> He was marvelous in all his ways, and it was as if the Baal
> Shem Tov had come to life in him. . . .
> Enchanted by a wealth of traditions and tales, I felt truly at
> home in Mezbizh. That little town so distant from Warsaw
> and yet so near was the place to which my childish imagina-
> tion went on many journeys.[6]

The Apter Rav, after whom Heschel was named, was popu-
larly known as the "lover of Israel" (*'Ohev Yisra'el*), which is
the title of his book and the sole inscription on his grave.
A story that Heschel's father told him as a boy about their
celebrated ancestor reflects a trait that has remained with the
Heschel family. When other Hasidic rabbis would ask the
Apter how it was that his prayers were accepted while theirs

were not, he would answer, "You see, whenever some Jew comes to me and pours out his heart and tells me of his suffering, I have such compassion that a little hole is created in my heart. Since I have listened to a great many Jews with their anguish, there are a great many holes in my heart. I'm an old Jew, and when I start to pray I take my heart and place it before God. He sees this broken heart, so many holes, so many tears, that He has compassion for my heart, and that's why He listens to me. He listens to my prayers."[7]

It can be said with certainty that the years in Warsaw provided that nourishment of spirit and intellect, that inner dignity of who he was, that gave permanent direction to Heschel's life. It could not, however, prevent him from peering beyond and, in the end, setting out from his home to explore the world of Western civilization that thundered and glittered about him.

Departing from Warsaw at eighteen, he traveled first to Vilna, where he pursued his secular education at the Yiddish Real-Gymnasium and joined a promising group of young Yiddish poets; then on to Berlin in 1927, the metropolis of science and philosophy in the twenties, where he immersed himself in the culture of the West, and began to absorb the rich offerings of art, music, philosophic thought, and scientific method.

He claimed he was no longer a Hasid. He had indeed abandoned their style of dress and their restricted social contacts for the larger world, both Jewish and German. But somehow Hasidism remained within Heschel:

> In my childhood and in my youth, I was the recipient of many blessings. I lived in the presence of quite a number of extraordinary persons I could revere. And just as I lived as a child in their presence, their presence continues to live in me as an adult. And yet I am not just a dwelling place for other people, an echo of the past. . . . I disagree with those who think of the present in the past tense. . . . The greatest danger is to become obsolete. I try not to be stale. I try to remain young. I have one talent and that is the capacity to be tremendously surprised, surprised at life, at ideas. This is to me the supreme Hasidic imperative.[8]

Later he gave a memorable description of the conflict he experienced between Berlin and Warsaw, between the intellectual claim of the university and the way of Torah:

> I came with great hunger to the University of Berlin to study philosophy. I looked for a system of thought, for the depth of the spirit, for the meaning of existence. Erudite and profound scholars gave courses in logic, epistemology, esthetics, ethics and metaphysics. . . .
>
> Yet, in spite of the intellectual power and honesty which I was privileged to witness, I became increasingly aware of the gulf that separated my views from those held at the university. . . . To them, religion was a feeling. To me, religion included the insights of the Torah which is a vision of man from the point of view of God. They spoke of God from the point of view of man. To them God was an idea, a postulate of reason. They granted Him the status of being a logical possibility. But to assume that He had existence would have been a crime against epistemology. . . .
>
> In those months in Berlin I went through moments of profound bitterness. I felt very much alone with my own problems and anxieties. I walked alone in the evenings through the magnificent streets of Berlin. I admired the solidity of its architecture, the overwhelming drive and power of a dynamic civilization. There were concerts, theatres, and lectures by famous scholars about the latest theories and inventions, and I was pondering whether to go to the new Max Reinhardt play or to a lecture about the theory of relativity.
>
> Suddenly I noticed the sun had gone down, evening had arrived. . . .
>
> I had forgotten God—I had forgotten Sinai—I had forgotten that sunset is my business—that my task is "to restore the world to the kingship of the Lord."
>
> So I began to utter the words of the evening prayer.
>
> *Blessed art thou, Lord our God,*
> *King of the universe,*
> *who by His word brings on the evenings. . . .*
>
> On that evening in the streets of Berlin, I was not in a mood to pray. My heart was heavy, my soul was sad. It was difficult for the lofty words of prayer to break through the dark clouds of my inner life.

But how would I dare not to *pray*? How would I dare to
miss an evening prayer?[9]

With Hitler's ascendancy to power and the tightening of the
Nazi tentacles, the young Heschel made rapid steps to establish his uncertain career. Though he arrived in Berlin only
in 1927, he published in rapid order a series of impressive
works: in 1933 his Yiddish poetry; in 1935 his biography of
Maimonides (along with receiving his doctorate from the
University of Berlin); in 1936 his important study on prophecy, which received an enthusiastic reception in scholarly
journals; in 1937 his brief work on Abravanel. He had just
reached thirty years of age. Meanwhile, his frequent articles
for the weekly of the Berlin Jewish community supple-
mented his meager income as a part-time editor at the Reiss
Verlag and as instructor in Talmud at the Hochschule, en-
abling him to contribute to the support of his mother and
sisters in Warsaw. In 1938 he moved to Frankfurt, chosen by
Martin Buber, who had left for Israel, as his successor as director of an area-wide program of Jewish studies, important
for the spiritual defense of the German Jews. When he had
been there for a year and a half, Heschel, along with all Polish Jews in Germany, was expelled back to Poland. He taught
at the modern rabbinical academy in Warsaw, from which
he was able to flee weeks before the Nazi invasion thanks to
a call from the Hebrew Union College in Cincinnati, Ohio.
After half a decade there, he spent the rest of his life in his
small, crowded study at the Jewish Theological Seminary in
New York from which his works emanated and to which
many made pilgrimage.

In Eastern Europe Heschel acquired ancestral Jewish
learning and piety; in Vilna, appreciation for secular Yiddish
culture; in Berlin, philosophy, method, and European culture. In Frankfurt he witnessed the fruitful synthesis of Jewish tradition and European culture. In America, with the
blessings of the free society that he cherished, the full extent
of his powers was reached. But wherever Heschel's feet took
him they always pointed toward Jerusalem.

Heschel was intimately familiar with the Jewries among whom he lived. It was the Warsaw-born Hasid, Abraham Heschel, who was chosen to write the introduction to the Lazer Ran's massive three-volume work on Vilna. Eugen Täubler, Mommsen's successor as professor of classics at Heidelberg, remarked to me that Heschel had a better grasp of German culture than the German-born faculty of the American academic institution in which Täubler found himself in the 1940s. Heschel not only understood the major Jewries of Europe and America, but also was thoroughly conversant with their cultures. He soon came to appreciate the pragmatic, open, and socially oriented American society that he encountered after his arrival in 1940, and for which, in time, he served as a leading spokesman. "You cannot realize," he once remarked to me, "what it means to be able to cast a ballot without fear. Americans do not sufficiently appreciate their country." Some questioned whether his enthusiastic political views were adopted with the same thorough understanding of the issues he demanded of himself in his strictly Jewish writings.

Scholarship

If the worlds of his environment were universal, so were the worlds of his *scholarship*.

Our age is one in which scholars know more and more about less and less. Heschel's genius embraced a number of fields. His interests were not limited to a single epoch or subject area. Vertically, there was hardly a major topic in the history of Jewish thought that he did not plumb. He wrote, among others, seminal works on the Bible: *The Prophets, Die Prophetie* (German); the Talmud: *The Theology of Ancient Judaism*, three volumes (Hebrew); biography: *Maimonides*; medieval thought: Saadia, Gabirol, etc.; theology: *Man Is Not Alone* and *God in Search of Man*; Hasidism: *A Passion for Truth, The Circle of the Baal Shem Tov*, and *Kotzk*, two volumes (Yiddish); contemporary moral issues: *The Insecurity of Freedom*; and poetry: *Man: The Ineffable Name of God* (Yid-

dish). He was a theologian, a poet, a mystic, a social re-
former, and an historian. Indeed, the best of the whole
tradition of Israel, its way of thought and life, found a unique
synthesis in him. It was this mastery of virtually the entire
range of Jewish creative experience, as well as much of
Western culture, that contributed to the richness of his
thinking. He was equally gifted in four languages—Yiddish,
Hebrew, German, and English—and would select in which
language he would write a book according to its subject.
Poetry and Hasidism in Yiddish, theology and ethics in English (and German), and rabbinics in Hebrew.

What Heschel wrote of Maimonides—that his "achievements . . . seem so incredible that one is almost inclined to
believe that Maimonides is the name of a whole academy of
scholars rather than the name of an individual!"[10]—reminds
one of Heschel himself.

Such scholarship had two requirements, at least: a lucid
mind and a determined will. Heschel possessed both. He accepted the old Jewish view that "Living is not a private affair
of the individual. Living is what man does with God's time,
what man does with God's world. . . ." "Life is a mandate,
not the enjoyment of an annuity; a task, not a game; a command, not a favor."[11] For the scholar this means never wast-
ing precious hours or energy. Petty controversy, for example,
was to be avoided at all costs. Once, after an unpleasant attack by a critic, he told me a story about his uncle, a famed
Warsaw rabbi. During a nasty dispute between his own Hasidic sect and another, he remained silent to all appeals for
support. When asked why, he quoted the Talmud: "The
fence around wisdom is silence. But," he added, "silence is
only the fence; what is the wisdom? The wisdom is that
petty controversy does not even concern me!"

Heschel admonished me not to forget the tale.

Heschel's immense productivity, despite his having been
uprooted twice from his cultural milieu, was not unrelated
to his understanding that, with the demise of East European
Jewry, he remained one of the few who could leave the record of what had been and what it should mean to future

generations. He felt a solemn burden: to pass this legacy on
to the next generation. How dare one waste valuable time?
"A world has vanished. All that remains is a sanctuary hidden
in the realm of spirit. We of this generation are still holding
the key. Unless we remember, unless we unlock it, the holiness of ages will remain a secret of God. . . . We are either
the last Jews or those who will hand over the entire past to
generations to come."[12] Heschel, above all, held that key.
And he lived with the knowledge that he held it.

Concern

In addition to the worlds of his environment and his scholarship, the worlds of Heschel's *concern* were likewise universal,
bridging the divisions that tend to divide. If his scholarship
moved readily across the vertical dimension from the Bible
to contemporary thought, his Jewish concern was just as remarkably horizontal. By this I mean his understanding of,
sympathy for, and acceptance by almost the entire spectrum
of Jewish life—from the Zionists, the Hebraists, and the Yid-
dishists to the artists, writers, and social activists; from the
Reform and Conservative to the Orthodox and the Hasidim. Though eschewing labels, identifying wholly with
none of these schools, and all the while holding his own
views, Heschel established good relations with each of the
factions, since he believed each represented, in greater or
lesser measure, an affirmation of Jewish life. His breadth expressed the quality of his *'ahavat Yisra'el* (love of Israel).
    Heschel reached out a hand to those of other faiths be-
cause of the depth, not the shallowness, of his own spiritual
life: the deeper the roots, the broader the branches. Or, as
one Christian scholar noted, "Heschel was most human as
he was most Jewish."[13] His ecumenical call was grounded in
his belief that human life partakes in the life of God; that
human beings dwell both in the realm of nature and in the
dimension of the holy; that the divine image, not only the
chromosome and the circulatory system, is the common
bond of humankind. Beneath the divisiveness of creeds lie

those underpinnings of religion, such as humility, compassion, awe, and faith, which characterize the community of all true persons of spirit. "Different are the languages of prayer," he wrote, "but the tears are the same."[14]

Heschel acted upon the spiritual fraternity of humankind in his ecumenical relations. His effort to nurture this bond was responded to so warmly by others because their spirits as well as their minds were engaged. He knew that if the divine fellowship did not enjoin us, a demonic one would. While some are "wary of the ecumenical movement," he wrote, "there is another ecumenical movement, worldwide in influence: nihilism. We must choose between interfaith and inter-nihilism."[15]

> No religion is an island. We are all involved with one another. Spiritual betrayal on the part of one of us affects the faith of all of us. Views adopted in one community have an impact on other communities. Today religious isolationism is a myth. . . . Should we refuse to be on speaking terms with one another and hope for each other's failure? Or should we pray for each other's health, and help one another in preserving one's respective legacy, in preserving a common legacy?[16]

An example of how Heschel was perceived by gentiles comes from a letter of an executive of the Bell System. He told how, in the 1960s, this corporation had an arrangement with Dartmouth College whereby each summer fifteen of its more promising middle managers spent eight weeks in Hanover, New Hampshire, studying the humanities and meeting special guests invited for a twenty-four–hour period. In the summer of 1964, Heschel was such a guest. Despite the passage of a decade and a half, Heschel's theme—the dignity, uniqueness, and sacredness of being human—was still fresh in his mind. Of his encounter with Heschel, the executive wrote:

> You must understand that the Bell System group was made up of middle-aged, gentile business executives, whose normal concerns were those of the corporation, and yet each member of the group was, I remember, struck by the aura of rever-

ence, wisdom, and concern for mankind which seemed to emanate from Rabbi Heschel. In my own case, I felt that his thoughts were communicated to me through a medium far beyond his words. If, when he had finished, he had risen and beckoned me to follow, I would have done so without questions. Even after 15 years, I am convinced that, on that day, I sat with a Biblical prophet.[17]

Heschel's environment, his scholarship, and his concern were each characterized by an unusually broad range. This contributed to the wholeness of his person: the breadth of his understanding as well as its depth.

NASI: A PRINCE OF HIS PEOPLE

If the sages of the Talmud were correct in saying that Israel's teachers are its royalty, then Heschel, the preeminent Jewish teacher of our generation, was a *nasi*, a prince of his people. Indeed, he was elected to high office as much by others as by his own.

His Importance for Catholics, Protestants, and Muslims

Rooted in the most authentic sources of Israel's faith, Heschel's audience reached beyond creedal boundaries. In the 1950s and 1960s, he was easily the most respected Jewish voice for Protestants and Catholics. His friendship with Reinhold Niebuhr was memorable, and his crucial role at Vatican II has yet to be fully described.

Catholics   A token of the esteem in which Catholics held Heschel is evident from the fact that among the tributes accorded him after his death in 1972 was an entire issue of *America* magazine devoted to his memory, unusual in any case and duplicated for no other Jew. The years since his passing, far from dimming his person, have cast in even brighter relief the unique role he played on the contemporary scene, a role no Jew, or gentile for that matter, has since filled.

His pervasive influence was felt at Vatican Council II, which was to review Catholic–Jewish relations in the form of a schema on the Jews. Asked by Cardinal Bea to draw up a proposal, Heschel composed a document that has served as a guideline for Catholics. Heschel traveled to Rome several times, where he argued for the Church's acceptance of "the permanent preciousness of the Jewish people," which meant the abandonment of its mission to the Jews and the recognition of its role in history. Heschel's efforts at Vatican II were of enormous significance. Moreover, he left a deep impression in Italy. He made a lecture tour there in conjunction with the Vatican; his books were translated into Italian, and he is, I believe, the only Jewish thinker to be quoted by a pope in this century.[18]

Several major Catholic-authored studies on Heschel's thought have been written, and a number of conferences have been sponsored. The most memorable was the one at a Catholic college in Minnesota in 1983, in preparation for which all students were required to read one or more of Heschel's works. The conference ran for three days and, in addition to kosher food and a formidable list of lecturers, featured the symphonic concert of a piece composed in Heschel's honor. At that gathering a faculty department head told me that she prayed to Heschel!

Two episodes may help to illustrate Heschel's unique relationship to the Catholic community:

One afternoon in the 1960s Heschel told me that he had just received a delegation of nuns. Their order was considering whether or not to give up their formal, longer habit for shorter, less cumbersome clothing. "What did you advise?" I asked. "I told them that such a personal matter should be settled by themselves." "But what is your opinion?" I persisted. "I do not believe they should change," he replied.

How unusual that the nuns should have come to him at all with such a request!

Once, while walking past St. Patrick's Cathedral, a Jew (Dr. Shlomo Noble of the YIVO) noticed in progress a protest demonstration against the war in Vietnam, where Cardinal Cooke had gone to support the military mission. While the Jew took a leaflet and put a few coins on the tray, the young boy who had handed him the tract looked at him, and then, trying to make contact, said hesitantly, "I know Rabbi Heschel."[19]

That name bridged the gap between a Catholic boy and the Jewish world.

Protestants   The Protestants also valued their link with Heschel. The most influential Protestant thinker in America in this century, Reinhold Niebuhr, placed him for the first time before the American reading public when, on the front page of the Sunday *New York Herald Tribune Book Review* of April 1, 1951, discussing Heschel's first major work, *Man Is Not Alone*, he wrote: "Abraham Heschel is one of the treasuries of spirit by which the persecutions, unloosed in Europe, inadvertently enriched our American culture. . . . He will become a commanding and authoritative voice not only in the Jewish community but in the religious life of America."[20]

Years later (1965–1966), Heschel became the first Jewish professor at the Union Theological Seminary in New York. Shortly after his death, I saw a handwritten letter on his desk from a noted Protestant which began with the salutation: "Dear Father Abraham"! And in his column in *The Christian Century* Martin Marty wrote: "Ha[s] the death of anyone since Pope John moved us so much . . . ?"[21]

Muslims   And the Muslims came to deeply respect Heschel. In 1972, some months before his death and against doctor's orders, Heschel attended a hitherto unpublicized conference in Rome. "It was the first occasion since the establishment of the State of Israel—and the last—that religious and other leaders of the three faiths involved in Jerusalem had met together to define the religious content of their devotion to the Holy City."[22] The conference had been proposed by the Anglican archbishop of Jerusalem and was sponsored by the Center for Mediterranean Studies in Rome, in cooperation with the Friends and the Jerusalem Foundation, "to explore the religious dynamics of the Jeru-

salem problem by attempting to define the spiritual necessi-
ties embedded in each of the three religions involved with
the city."[23] It was their hope that political considerations
might be influenced by the "devout and profound personalities present."[24]

Archbishop Appleton opened each day's discussion with
prayers, and a reading was given by each of the different
faiths. Heschel was invited to read for the Jews. Observing
that the coming Sabbath immediately preceded Rosh Hashana, the Jewish New Year, he recited the prophetical por-
tion from Isaiah assigned for that Sabbath in the synagogue
liturgy:

> For Zion's sake will I not hold my peace,
> And for Jerusalem's sake I will not rest. . . .
> I have set watchmen upon thy walls, O Jerusalem,
> They shall never hold their peace day nor night:
> "Ye that are the Lord's remembrances,
> Take ye no rest, and give Him no rest,
> Till He establish, and till He make Jerusalem
> A praise in the earth. . . ."
> For He said: "Surely, they are My people,
> Children that will not deal falsely. . . ."
> In all their affliction He was afflicted,
> And the angel of His presence saved them;
> And He bore them, and carried them all the days
> of old (Is. 62:1, 2, 4, 5–7; 63:8–9).

After the ecumenical service had concluded, Heschel visibly
moved the Muslims by remarking that, "It is important for
me to remember now, that, while I have prayed from the
heart for the Muslims all my life, I have never prayed with
them before, or been face-to-face with them to talk about
God. This is so important. We must go further."[25]

Heschel believed that seemingly insoluble problems, even
one so hoary and complex as Jerusalem, could be resolved if
a spiritual understanding were first achieved. He trusted that
even during those few meetings a "common language
among the religions could be found."[26] Summarizing the
conference, the Center director, E. A. Bayne, wrote me. "In

such a setting Rabbi Heschel performed superbly as we had
hoped. Although [he was] fragile in health, his spirit never
flagged. . . . Largely because of his presence, I believe, in
support of the spiritual dimension of the inquiry, the seminar
was rewarding. . . . Had we the funds, however, another
session could have been fruitful, if not definitive; but it was
not to be."[27]

At the close of the final meeting, Heschel, who moved
slowly in those days, shuffled toward the door with only
the two Muslim Khadis apparently remaining behind. One
approached him, squeezed his hand, and departed. The second took his hand and said: "I have read all that you have
written. God bless your work."

The Blacks

A picture that should hang in black and Jewish homes is that
of Heschel and Martin Luther King marching arm-in-arm in
Selma, Alabama, an event Heschel recalled in typically striking summation: "When I marched in Selma, I felt that my
legs were praying." Not only did Heschel and King march
together, they also had profound respect for each other as
well. Shortly before King's assassination, Heschel said of
him: "Martin Luther King is a sign that God has not forsaken
the United States of America. God has sent him to us. . . .
His mission is sacred. . . . I call upon every Jew to hearken
to his voice, to share his vision, to follow in his way. The
whole future of America will depend upon the . . . influence
of Dr. King."[28]

Describing Heschel as "one of the great men of our age, a
truly great prophet," King recognized his contribution to
the Civil Rights Movement: "He has been with us in many
struggles. I remember marching from Selma to Montgom-
ery, how he stood at my side. . . . I remember very well
when we were in Chicago for the Conference on Religion
and Race. . . . his speech inspired clergymen of all faiths . . .
to do something that they had not done before."[29]

In that historic speech to which King referred, given in

1963 at the initial Conference on Religion and Race in Chicago, Heschel's opening words startled his audience and
helped to set the stage for the momentous changes that were
to come:

> At the first conference on religion and race, the main partici-
> pants were Pharaoh and Moses. Moses' words were: "Thus
> says the Lord, the God of Israel, let My people go that they
> may celebrate a feast to Me." While Pharaoh retorted: "Who
> is the Lord that I should heed His voice and let Israel go? . . ."
> The outcome of that summit meeting has not come to an
> end. Pharaoh is not ready to capitulate. The exodus began,
> but is far from having been completed. . . . The Negro move-
> ment is an outcry of pain in which a sickness of our total
> society comes to the expression. . . . It is the problem of
> jobs for the disemployed, dignity for those who are on relief,
> employment for the unskilled, the threat of automation, the
> curse of poverty, the blighted slums in our cities.[30]

By 1984 the black–Jewish coalition from the civil rights era,
which had been ailing throughout the 1970s, came to an end
as the Rev. Jesse Jackson, a Baptist preacher like King, started
to preach a very different sermon to the Jewish community.
During the warmer days of their relationship, some blacks
had believed Jews were not "white," as many Jews had believed that blacks were not "goyim." But attitudes changed,
and blacks began to see Jews, who had advanced on the ladder of financial success, not only as whites but as super–
scapegoat-whites. Jews, for their part, saw that some blacks
were capable of such anti-Semitism as to be branded "super-
goyim."

Jewish support for the civil rights movement began cool-
ing as discrimination "for" blacks replaced discrimination
against them; affirmative action shifted from "equal opportunity," its original intent, into strict "quotas," and honest
competition was replaced by a massive government-sup-
ported spoils system. A black candidate—instead of the Ku
Klux Klan—injected anti-Semitism into the 1984 presiden-
tial campaign. For both blacks and Jews, the anti-Semitic
aspect of the Jackson phenomenon was a danger signal. As it

had once refused to disavow the Ku Klux Klan in the 1924 campaign, so in the 1984 campaign, the Democratic Party's "failure to repudiate by name, loud and clear, the purveyors of racist antisemitism" showed that anti-Jewish bigotry had "voter appeal." In the 1990s, far from disavowal, overtures of cooperation were extended by the NAACP, the Congressional Black Caucus, and others to the charismatic spokesman of a far more vicious antisemitism, that of "minister" Farrakan.

Still, as late as 1983, when a conference was convened to confront black–Jewish relations, it was structured around the personalities of Heschel and King. By examining their lives and teachings, it was hoped that a common spiritual ground might be explored, out of which a constructive dialogue on sensitive issues could grow.

Champion of the Poor and the Aged

The eloquence of Heschel's voice and the power of his word were heard again and again on behalf of the neglected and the forlorn. He once said he was propelled out of the security of the ivory tower of research into the swirling domain of public issues because of his study of the prophets. "Prophecy," he wrote, "is the voice that God has lent to the silent agony, a voice to the plundered poor. . . . God is raging in the prophets' words."[31] In Heschel's voice an echo of that rage was heard.

Abraham Joshua Heschel was, as well, the most effective spokesman on behalf of the aged. In 1961, the first White House Conference on Aging found some six thousand delegates in attendance. Hundreds of sessions took place, and countless papers from noted authorities were given. However, one address—Heschel's—so impressed the assembly that it was selected as the single representative statement for the conference and appeared in the *Congressional Record*, as well as on the official recording, whose other side contains the address of President Eisenhower. These are the closing words of Heschel's speech:

We must seek ways to overcome the traumatic fear of being old, the prejudice, the discrimination against those advanced in years. All men are created equal, including those advanced in years. Being old is not necessarily the same as being stale. The effort to restore the dignity of old age will depend upon our ability to revive the equation of old age and wisdom. Wisdom is the substance upon which the inner security of the old will forever depend. But the attainment of wisdom is the work of a life time.

> Old men need a vision, not only recreation.
> Old men need a dream, not only a memory.
> It takes three things to attain a sense of significant being:
>   God
>   A Soul
>   And a Moment.
> And these three are always here.
> Just to be is a blessing. Just to live is holy.[32]

The Struggle for Soviet Jewry

The Russian Jews were grateful to Heschel.

He was among the first to alert us to the calamity in those early years when few were aware of it. (He urged Elie Wiesel to travel to Russia, the result of which was his book *The Jews of Silence*—Jews, that is, who speak out of fear, in silence, with their eyes.) Heschel's plea on behalf of Russian Jews led to rescue efforts that brought thousands into freedom. Heschel used to remind us that the Russian Jews will do more for us than we will ever do for them. He was referring to the courageous example of those who persisted as Jews for seventy-five years without synagogues, religious schools or books, and against the vicious anti-religious and anti-Semitic apparatus of the Soviet government.

In an early address he compared modern Jewry's attitude toward the Russian Jews to the stance of ancient Jewry toward the Ten Lost Tribes:

One of the tragic failures of ancient Judaism was the indifference of our people to the Ten Tribes of Israel which were

carried away into exile by Assyria after the Northern Kingdom of Samaria was destroyed. Uncared for, unattended to,
overlooked and abandoned, the Ten Tribes were consigned
to oblivion. . . . At the end, they vanished. . . .

There is a nightmare that terrifies me today: the unaware-
ness of our being involved in a new failure, in a tragic derelic-
tion of duty.

East European Jewry vanished. Russian Jewry is the last
remnant of a people destroyed in extermination camps, the
last remnant of a spiritual glory that is no more. . . . Let the
twentieth century not enter the annals of Jewish history as the
century of physical and spiritual destruction.[33]

The Six Million

The Jews of Europe, living and dead, had in Heschel their
most persuasive spokesman. His inaugural address at The
Union Theological Seminary before a distinguished body of
Christian leaders, began:

> I speak as a member of a congregation whose founder was
> Abraham, and the name of my Rabbi is Moses. I speak as a
> person who was able to leave Warsaw, the city in which I was
> born, just six weeks before the disaster began. My destination
> was New York; it would have been Auschwitz or Treblinka.
> I am a brand plucked from the fire, in which my people was
> burned to death. I am a brand plucked from the fire of an
> altar of Satan on which millions of human lives were extermi-
> nated to evil's greater glory, and on which so much else was
> consumed: the divine image of so many human beings, many
> people's faith in the God of justice and compassion, and much
> of the secret and power of attachment to the Bible bred and
> cherished in the hearts of men for nearly 2,000 years.[34]

I saw Heschel almost daily from the end of 1942 to 1945,
but rarely did he discuss with me what must have grieved
him most, the end of the thousand-year period of East European Jewry, which he called "the golden period of Jewish
history."[35] An interview with the Yiddish journalist Gershon
Jacobson in 1963 reveals his frustrating efforts in behalf of
his dying people.

"I was an immigrant, a refugee. No one listened to me. In 1941 I met with a prominent Jewish communal leader, a devoted Zionist. I told him that the Jews of the Warsaw ghetto endure in the belief that American Jewry is working ceaselessly on their behalf. Were they to know of our indifference, the Jews in Warsaw would perish from shock. My words fell on deaf ears. In 1942 [or 1941] I was at a convention of Reform rabbis. A representative of the Quakers appeared, demanding that the rabbis adopt a resolution to have food parcels sent to the Jews in the ghettos and concentration camps. The appeal was turned down. The rabbis explained that they could not do it officially, because it might aid the Germans by sending food into their territory. In 1943 I attended the American Jewish Conference, which encompassed all major Jewish organizations in the country, to appeal that they act to extinguish the flames which had engulfed Eastern European Jewry. The Conference had a long agenda—Eretz-Yisrael, fascism, finances, etc.—the last item of which was Jews under the Germans. By the time they reached this issue, almost all the representatives had left. I went away brokenhearted."

"What did you do then," asked Jacobson?

"I went to Rabbi Eliezer Silver's synagogue in Cincinnati [Silver was actively involved in saving Jews during the Holocaust], recited Psalms, fasted, and cried myself out. I was a stranger in this country. My word had no power. When I did speak, they shouted me down. They called me a mystic, unrealistic. I had no influence on leaders of American Jewry."[36]

Instead of describing the horror—the "Holocaust"—he preferred to write about what was most enduring from that golden era—its beauty, its meaning, its holiness. He delivered an unforgettable eulogy to the six million in his book *The Earth Is the Lord's*, in which he sketched the lasting values of East European Jewry, and wrote during the war years while he was still in Cincinnati. He referred me to a short story, written by a friend of his, in which a Hasidic master warned his disciples, in the name of sanity, not to dwell overmuch upon the horrors that were to come, citing as

proof the Book of Exodus, in which only the first few chapters deal with the sufferings of slavery, while the preponder-
ance of the volume dwells upon the "going out from
Egypt," the "exodus."[37] Of course, we need both records—
the Holocaust and the holiness. But it was the way of
Heschel to choose the affirmative portrayal of the noble. Of
East European Jewry, he wrote: "The little Jewish communities in Eastern Europe were like sacred texts opened before
the eyes of God, so close were their houses of worship to
Mount Sinai. In the humble wooden synagogues, looking as
if they were deliberately closing themselves off from the
world, the Jews purified the souls that God had given them.
. . . They did not write songs, they themselves were songs."[38]
The liquidation of East-European Jewry left Heschel as one
of the few authentic interpreters of that great period of Jewish life and thought.

ZADDIK OF THE GENERATION

I have said that Heschel was a *nasi*, a prince of his people,
and *shalem*, a whole person. He was, finally, a *zaddik*.

Behind his public face as thinker, writer, and advocate,
was a private undisclosed frame—the zaddik, the Hasidic
master, that remarkable new leader who emerged from the
movement of Hasidism, and who renewed the life of eigh-
teenth- and nineteenth-century East European Jewry.
Heschel must be understood, in good measure, against the
pattern of those masters. Since succession in Hasidic leadership was dynastic, Heschel, as a member of that royalty, had
been raised to sit upon the zaddik's throne, as his father and
his father's father had done before. Indeed, of him even
more was expected. And yet, though he abdicated his destined role by departing for the West, that is what he ulti-
mately became: the zaddik of his generation.[39]

To read Heschel is to peer into the heart of that rarest of
human phenomena, the holy man. For he was one of those
who experienced the presence of the living God, before

Whom he walked in the seclusion of prayer and study as well as in the maelstrom of public life. He represented what Gershom Scholem described as the paradox of the zaddik: isolation and communion, to live a public life and yet to be alone with God. To Heschel the question of religion "is not 'what man does with his solitariness,' " but "what man does with the presence of God":[40] how to think, feel, act; how to live in a way that is compatible with our being a likeness of God; how to be what one is; how to so conduct ourselves that our lives can be an answer to God's question.

Entering his study one afternoon, I found Heschel weary from the visit of a self-centered Jewish thinker who enjoyed "talking" theology. Pensive, Heschel finally remarked to me: "One can only speak of God in the presence of God."

Sometime later, in an address to theologians, he said, "a theory of God can easily become a substitute for God, impressive to the mind when God as a living reality is absent from the soul."[41]

The zaddik was both scholar and pietist, master of prayer and teacher of Torah, bound up with God and the center of the community, wielder of power yet humble, a teacher by example as well as by word, one who affirmed life by celebrating it in joy, whose every act was meant to glorify God. The zaddik was meant not only to teach Torah but also to be Torah, a living Torah. His disciples were to learn from his life as well as from his words. When we consider Heschel's life and work against this description, we see how he approximated it.

Prayer, upon which the life of the zaddik centered, sustained Heschel's rich inner life. The analysis of prayer that he has given us is as profound as any we possess. That analysis—descriptive, analytical, poetic, suggestive—is surely, in part, personal.

Prayer is *spiritual ecstasy*. It is as if all our vital thoughts in fierce ardor would burst the mind to stream toward God. A keen single force draws our yearning for the utmost out of the seclusion of the soul. We try to see our visions in His light, to feel our life as His affair. We begin by letting the thought of Him engage our minds, by realizing His name and entering into a reverie which leads through beauty and stillness, from feeling to thought, and from understanding to devotion.[42]

In the mid-1940s, Heschel initiated me into the regimen of daily worship. I would join him in his room at dawn to pray the morning service. Those were unforgettable hours. With his large prayer shawl about him and his tefillin on his head and arm, he paced the room reciting the long pages by heart, at first slowly and softly but then more quickly and loudly, the words flowing as a torrent from him, at times roaring like a lion, rising at last to a culmination of motionless silence, all within. Time opened to eternity.

The task of the zaddik was to seek out the sparks of holiness everywhere, even amidst evil. This too was true of Heschel. He restrained himself from unnecessary criticism, even when under attack, preferring to dwell upon the virtues of others.

How sad, a student once remarked to him, that two Holocaust orphans would be bereft of family at their forthcoming wedding. How wonderful, Heschel corrected him, that two orphans, each with no one else, had found each other!

Isolation was anathema to the zaddik. Hasidic writers disparage Noah as the symbol of the unconcerned leader, because he "walked *with* God," that is, in such selfish seclusion that he, in effect, caused the flood; while Abraham was acclaimed as the symbol of the zaddik, because he walked "*before*" God "in the midst of the city" and would have prevented the deluge had he lived earlier.[43] Though Heschel was absorbed with his research and writing, his door was open to all. And they came, not only with problems of the intellect, but also with problems of life. Other scholars protected their privacy and were unavailable. Not so Heschel.

The zaddik stood for exalted leadership, for the Baal Shem Tov had taught that all could be changed by a true master. Heschel tried to convey the gravity of the rabbinic calling to his students. In class each year he would recall the answer that the German poet Rainer Maria Rilke gave to the young man who wrote, asking whether he should become a poet: "Only if you cannot live without being a poet!" That was Heschel's advice to incipient rabbis (or ministers): become a rabbi only if your life depends upon it. Heschel once told me that before his death Moses prayed for a worthy successor—"Let the Lord set a man over the congregation, who will go out before them and will come in before them . . . that the congregation of the Lord be not as sheep which have no shepherd" (Num. 27:18). To which Heschel cited the interpretation of the Hasidic master of Kotzk: To "go out before them" can be translated in Yiddish as *"ois-gehen far zey"*—one who is willing to die for them!

FROM METAPHYSICS TO HUMAN DEED

On the anniversary of the death of Albert Schweitzer, Heschel occasionally took class-time to review the latter's life: how he forsook glory as a famed philosopher, organist, and musicologist to become a common doctor in a clinic in deepest Africa as atonement for the sins of the white race.

One is reminded of the last chapter of his biography of Maimonides in which Heschel proposed a solution to a paradox that had long puzzled scholars. Maimonides, a colossus in philosophy, law, and science, wrote, for the most part, in the lingua franca of the time, Arabic, though he knew that only in Hebrew could his writings reach the entire Jewish people. Nevertheless, toward the end of his life, he advised his translator, Ibn Tibbon, by letter, not to take the long journey from Europe to visit him in Egypt, because he could spend little time with him even were he to come. There follows an exhausting itinerary of Maimonides' schedule of daily medical work from early dawn to late evening with time only for a single meal. Why? Why did he forsake his momentous unfinished scholarly projects to heal the sick, which any doctor could have done? Heschel suggests an answer: "This is Maimonides' last metamorphosis: From meta-

physics to medicine, from contemplation to practice, from
speculation to the imitation of God. . . . Preoccupation with
the concrete man and the effort to aid him in his suffering is
now the form of religious devotion. . . . Personal achieve-
ment is abandoned for the sake of enhancing God's presence
in human deeds. . . ."[44]

What Heschel said of Maimonides might once again be
said of himself. Despite the frailty of his health and the projects yet to be completed and the books yet to be written—
The Baal Shem Tov, a "Midrash Rabba" of Hasidism,
biblical versus Greek thinking, The Shema, The Day of
Atonement, etc.—he spent more and more time in the last
years of his life on such social issues as civil rights, the Vietnam war, and the plight of Russian Jewry.

Prayer had become deed.

Heschel's Two Hasidic Masters

According to his own testimony, two opposite Hasidic masters served as models to Heschel: The Baal Shem Tov, the
founder of Hasidism, and his counterpart, Rabbi Mendl of
Kotzk. About their influence on him, Heschel wrote:

The earliest fascination I can recall is associated with the Baal
Shem, whose parables disclosed some of the first insights I
gained as a child. He remained a model too sublime to follow
yet too overwhelming to ignore.

It was in my ninth year that the presence of Reb Menahem
Mendl of Kotzk, known as the Kotzker, entered my life.
Since then he has remained a steady companion and a haunt-
ing challenge. Although he often stunted me, he also urged
me to confront perplexities that I might have preferred to
evade.

Years later I realized that, in being guided by both the Baal
Shem Tov and the Kotzker, I had allowed two forces to carry
on a struggle within me. . . . The one reminded me that
there could be a Heaven on earth, the other shocked me into
discovering Hell in the alleged Heavenly places in our
world. . . .

The Baal Shem dwelled in my life like a lamp, while the
Kotzker struck like lightning.[45]

As in his philosophy, so in his life, a polarity of ways prevailed; the love, forgiveness, and gentleness of the Baal Shem
versus the Kotzker's uncompromising demand, his contempt
for fraud, his harsh manner, his fearless pursuit of truth.
From a master in the tradition of Kotzk, Heschel's words
were often like a hammer upon a rock: sparks lit up the
darkness of apathy.

To a conference of American religious leaders, Heschel
lamented:

> This is a time to cry out. One is ashamed to be human. One
> is embarrassed to be called religious in the face of religion's
> failure to keep alive the image of God in the face of man. . . .
> Religion declined not because it was refuted, but because it
> became irrelevant, dull, oppressive, insipid. . . . We have im-
> prisoned God in our sanctuaries and slogans, and now the
> word of God is dying on our lips. . . . There is darkness in the
> East, and smugness in the West. What of the night? What of
> the night?[46]

Heschel chided rabbis lest they fall into one of two camps:
those who are willing to kill every Jew for a din (a religious
law), and those who are willing to kill every din for a Jew.
Reform rabbis were reproached for their prejudice against
the Law: "Let us beware lest we reduce Bible to literature,
Jewish observance to good manners, the Talmud to Emily
Post."[47] The Orthodox were cautioned against an "all or
nothing" approach: "The intransigent refuse to surrender a
single iota, yet are ready to surrender the multitudes of Israel";[48] while Conservatives were stunned to be challenged
as to whether the temple has "become the graveyard where
prayer is buried. . . . There are many who labor in the vine-
yard of oratory; but who knows how to pray, or how to
inspire others to pray? . . . The modern temple suffers from
a severe cold. . . . Our motto is monotony. The fire has gone
out of our worship. It is cold, stiff, and dead. . . . the rabbi
[has become] a master of ceremonies" but "Judaism does not
stand on ceremonies. . . ."[49]

Before Jewish educators, Heschel attacked the popular notion of self-expression. "Self-expression depends upon self-
attachment to what is greater than the self. . . . There must
be something to be expressed, an emotion, a vision, an end.
. . . everything depends on the person who stands in the
front of the classroom. . . . To guide a pupil into the promised land, he [the teacher] must have been there himself. . . .
What we need more than anything else is not *textbooks* but
textpeople."[50]

At a American Medical Association convention in San
Francisco, he warned that medicine itself was in need of
therapy, that while "[m]edicine is a sacred art," too many
doctors had become plumbers, and that sickness was not
only a physical disorder but a "crisis of the total person." He
spoke of the "nightmare of medical bills," and berated them
for creating a "*Sisyphus complex*," by curing the patient phys-
ically while destroying him economically.[51] The following
day the San Francisco paper ran a banner: "Dr. Heschel's
Bitter Pill"!

Few were to depart from such lectures unchanged. The
searing words were in the spirit of the master of Kotzk.

But even more than a cry for justice, one heard from
Heschel a call to grandeur, to compassion, to hope, a song
of celebration and exaltation. It was the voice of the other,
still greater master: the Baal Shem Tov.

"The universe is not a waif and life is not a derelict. Man
is neither the lord of the universe nor even the master of his
own destiny. Our life is not our own property but a possession of God. And it is this divine ownership that makes life
a sacred thing."[52]

Or—"We live by the conviction that acts of goodness reflect the hidden light of His holiness. His light is above our
minds but not beyond our will. It is within our power to
mirror His unending love in deeds of kindness, like brooks
that hold the sky."[53]

Again—"The world of things we perceive is but a veil. Its
flutter is music, its ornament science, but what it conceals is
inscrutable. Its silence remains unbroken; no words can carry

it away. Sometimes we wish the world could cry and tell us about that which made it pregnant with fear-filling grandeur. Sometimes we wish our own heart would speak of that which made it heavy with wonder."[54]

For Jews, hearing and reading Heschel meant understanding, often for the first time, the message, and the glory, of their destiny: "Judaism is the track of God in the wilderness of oblivion. By being what we are, namely Jews; by attuning our own yearning to the lonely holiness in this world, we will aid humanity more than by any particular service we may render." For "[w]hat we do as individuals is a trivial episode; what we attain as Israel causes us to become a part of eternity."[55]

"[The people] Israel is the tree, we are the leaves. It is the clinging to the stem that keeps us alive. There has perhaps never been more need of Judaism than in our time, a time in which many cherished hopes of humanity lie crushed. We should be pioneers as were our fathers three thousand years ago. The future of all men depends upon their realizing that the sense of holiness is as vital as health. By following the Jewish way of life we maintain that sense and preserve the light for mankind's future visions."[56]

"We are God's stake in human history. We are the dawn and the dusk, the challenge and the test. How strange to be a Jew and go astray on God's perilous errands. We have been offered as a pattern of worship and as a prey for scorn, but there is more still in our destiny. We carry the gold of God in our souls to forge the gate of the kingdom. The time for the kingdom may be far off, but the task is plain: to retain our share in God in spite of peril and contempt. . . . Loyal to the presence of the ultimate in the common, we may be able to make it clear that man is more than man, that in doing the finite he may perceive the infinite."[57]

How could one hear such words and not listen to their echo, and re-echo, not ponder them, and be changed by them?

Who was Rabbi Abraham Joshua Heschel? He was a *nasi*,

a prince of his people; *shalem*, marvelously whole; *zaddik hador*, master for our age.

Notes

1. Quotations for which no sources are given come from my conversations with Heschel, or from family members.

2. Abraham Joshua Heschel, *Man Is Not Alone: A Philosophy of Religion* (New York: Farrar, Straus, & Young, 1951), pp. 295–96.

3. Susannah Heschel, in an address at a conference on Abraham Joshua Heschel sponsored by the Chicago Board of Jewish Education, February 20–21, 1983.

4. *Man Is Not Alone*, p. 282.

5. Abraham J. Heschel, *Man's Quest for God: Studies in Prayer and Symbolism* (New York: Charles Scribner's Sons, 1954), p. 147, from an address originally delivered in March 1938 at a conference of Quaker leaders in Frankfurt.

6. Abraham Joshua Heschel, *A Passion for Truth* (New York: Farrar, Straus, & Giroux, 1973; repr. New York: Noonday, 1974; Woodstock, Vt.: Jewish Lights Publishing, 1995), p. xiii.

7. Abraham Heschel, "Hasidism," *Jewish Heritage*, 14, No. 3 (1972), 21.

8. Abraham Joshua Heschel, "In Search of Exaltation," ibid., 13 (Fall 1971), 29, 30, 35.

9. *Man's Quest for God*, pp. 94, 95, 96, 97–98.

10. Abraham Joshua Heschel, *The Insecurity of Freedom* (New York: Schocken Books, 1966), p. 285.

11. Abraham Joshua Heschel, *God in Search of Man: A Philosophy of Judaism* (New York: Farrar, Straus, & Cudahy, 1955), p. 356; *Man Is Not Alone*, p. 294.

12. Abraham Joshua Heschel, *The Earth Is the Lord's: The Inner World of the Jew in East Europe* (New York: Henry Schuman, Inc., 1950), p. 107.

13. W. D. Davies, "Conscience, Scholar, Witness," *America*, 128 (March 10, 1973), p. 215.

14. *The Insecurity of Freedom*, p. 180.

15. Abraham Joshua Heschel, "No Religion Is an Island," *Union Seminary Quarterly Review*, 21 (January 1966), 119.

16. Ibid.

17. Letter from S. H. Washburn to Samuel H. Dresner, March 20, 1979.

18. Cf. "Editorial: Contemporary Judaism and the Christian," *America*, 128 (March 10, 1973), p. 202.

19. Personal communication, Shlomo Noble.

20. Reinhold Niebuhr, "Masterful Analysis of Faith," *New York Herald Tribune Book Review*, 118 (April 1, 1951), p. 12.

21. Martin Marty, *The Christian Century*, 19 (January 17, 1973), 87.

22. E. A. Bayne, pamphlet published by the Center for Mediterranean Studies in Rome, 1973.

23. Letter from E. A. Bayne to Samuel H. Dresner, December 29, 1982.

24. Ibid.

25. Bayne, pamphlet of the Center for Mediterranean Studies.

26. Ibid.

27. Bayne, letter to Samuel Dresner.

28. Abraham Joshua Heschel, quoted in *Conservative Judaism*, 22 (Spring 1968), 1.

29. Martin Luther King, Jr., quoted in *Conservative Judaism*, 22 (Spring 1968), 1.

30. *The Insecurity of Freedom*, p. 85.

31. Ibid., p. 11.

32. Ibid., p. 84.

33. Ibid., pp. 271, 273.

34. "No Religion Is an Island," 117.

35. *The Earth Is the Lord's*, p. 10.

36. *Day-Morning Journal*, June 13, 1963. I thank Dr. Zanvel Klein for calling this interview to my attention. Further evidence of Heschel's efforts is found in a letter of the talmudist Rabbi Levi Ginzberg, appended to a legal responsum to a prominent rabbi. "May I . . . ask of you a great favor. My friend and colleague, Doctor Abraham Heschel, told me that he had written to you asking you to use your influence with the HIAS [Hebrew Immigrant Aid Society]. Doctor Heschel is not only a great scholar, but a very close friend of mine, and any favor shown to him I would consider as shown to me" (E. Golinkin, ed., *The Responsa of Professor Louis Ginzberg* [New York: Jewish Theological Seminary, 1996]).

37. Cf. Fischel Schneirson, "Ani Maamin" ("I Believe"), translation Samuel H. Dresner, *Conservative Judaism*, 22 (Spring 1968), 20–30.

38. *The Earth Is the Lord's*, pp. 92–93.

39. Cf. Samuel H. Dresner, *The Zaddik* (London and New York: Abelard-Schuman, 1960; repr. New York: Schocken Books, 1974; Aronson, 1994). The day after Heschel's funeral the noted thinker Arthur Green told me that when in 1960 he first read the words of the dedication of my book—"To Abraham Joshua Heschel, . . . Zaddik Hador (Zaddik of the generation)"—he did not believe it. "Now," he concluded, "I know you were right."

40. *Man's Quest for God*, p. xiv.

41. Abraham Joshua Heschel, "The Jewish Notion of God and Christian Renewal," in *Renewal of Religious Thought*, vol. 1 of *Theology of Renewal*, ed. L. K. Shook (New York: Herder & Herder, 1968), p. 106; from an address to a congress of Catholic Theologians in Toronto, 1967.

42. *Man's Quest for God*, pp. 18–19.

43. Cf. Dresner, *The Zaddik*, chaps. 4 and 7.

44. *The Insecurity of Freedom*, pp. 289–90.

45. *A Passion for Truth*, pp. xiv, xv.

46. *The Insecurity of Freedom*, pp. 165, 3–4, 165.

47. *Man's Quest for God*, p. 113; from an address originally delivered in 1953 before the Central Conference of Conservative Rabbis.

48. *The Insecurity of Freedom*, p. 205; from an address entitled "The Individual Jew and His Obligations," delivered in 1957 at the Jerusalem Ideological Conference, convened at the Hebrew University.

49. *Man's Quest for God*, pp. 50, 49, 114.

50. *The Insecurity of Freedom*, pp. 64, 229, 237.

51. Ibid., pp. 33, 32, 35.

52. *Man Is Not Alone*, pp. 226–27.

53. *God in Search of Man*, p. 290.

54. *Man Is Not Alone*, p. 16.

55. *The Earth Is the Lord's*, p. 108; *Man's Quest for God*, p. 45.

56. *God in Search of Man*, p. 424.

57. *The Earth Is the Lord's*, p. 109.

2

Hasidism

HESCHEL'S ROOTS were in early twentieth-century Hasidism, of whose nobility he was one of the last, and perhaps the most eminent. Within the milieu of his family, it was still possible for him to feel the glow of the fire his forefathers had kindled centuries before, the fire Hitler's legions strove to stamp out or scatter asunder. Embarrassed by the twentieth-century's inability to produce a second Heschel, it is only natural for us to be curious as to Hasidism itself. That inquiry will lead us to several surprises.

Hasidism has been described as a revival movement, and revival movements do not as a rule endure. Not so Hasidism. Emerging in eighteenth-century Eastern Europe, it has continued down to our very day even in the most unexpected of places, despite repeated warnings as to its decay and imminent collapse. Fuel was somehow found to stoke the fires from time to time, so that the waves that broke upon the Hasidim could not extinguish the light. Neither the challenge of modern science and thought of the nineteenth century, nor the Communist suppression of the twentieth—not even the Nazi onslaught with its unparalleled destruction of their communities, their leaders, and their followers—sealed their doom. Hasidism not only has survived them all, but is undergoing a considerable revival in the lands of dispersion—America, Israel, and Europe. Even Americans are coming to recognize the difference between the black costumes of the Hasidim and those of the Amish, while politicians and reporters in New York have begun including them

An earlier version of this chapter appeared as the introduction to Abraham Joshua Heschel, *The Circle of the Baal Shem Tov: Studies in Hasidism*, ed. Samuel H. Dresner (Chicago: The University of Chicago Press, 1985; rev. ed. New York: Jewish Theological Seminary, 1998), pp. vii–xiv.

in the local ethnic power groups: there are the Asians, the Hispanics, and the "Hasidics."

American Jews who succeed in resisting the new paganism or in escaping from its clutches owe a debt of gratitude to the discovery of the spiritual riches of Hasidism, a world only recently made available to us through the efforts of Buber, Heschel, and others. It is almost axiomatic that the road leading to faith and *mitzvot* today must pass through the music, legends, teachings, and lives of the Hasidic masters.

What is the secret they possess?

The last great flowering of the Jewish spirit, Hasidism transformed the life of an eighteenth-century Polish Jewry. The shtetls in which East European Jews lived were cut off from the burgeoning worlds of philosophy, art, and commerce that were flourishing in the emancipated West. Modern man had welcomed the dawning of the new Age of Reason with trembling anticipation after having endured for so long the dark night of Faith, for central to his creed was the unshakable belief that the systematic use of man's reason would penetrate all mysteries, just as the responsible employment of freedom would mark the end of every tyranny. What could Hasidic truth, the parochial teachings of some benighted, superstitious Jews of the medieval East, possibly mean to those newly acculturated Jews of the West? What could it mean to the gentile? And what meaning can it possibly have for us of the twentieth-first century?

While it is to be regretted that Heschel's detailed monographs dealing with the circle of the Baal Shem Tov (ca. 1690–1760), the founder of the Hasidic movement, failed to lead to a full-length evaluation of the Baal Shem and his teachings, especially since Heschel's textual and historical studies were generally done not for their own sake but in order to distill the meaning of the material he researched, there are a number of scattered remarks in his notes, in his more popular writings, and in *A Passion for Truth* that point to what he wished eventually to say. Obviously, they must not be taken as his measured and scholarly view either of the movement or of the man who was its founder.

"Hasidism," Heschel writes, "was neither a sect nor a doctrine. It was a dynamic approach to reality. That was its essence. It succeeded in liquefying a frozen system of values and ideas. Everything was neatly labeled—good and evil, clean and unclean, safe and dangerous, rich and poor, *rasha'* and *tzaddik*, *mitzvah* and *'averah*, beautiful and ugly, truth and falsehood. But such a division is artificial. Life cannot be enclosed in boxes. Values are often ambiguous. What, for example, is beauty? Something in itself, or an experience born when a person who loves the beautiful discovers it? In attaching oneself to the source of all unity, the Hasid learned to bend every action to the ultimate goal. Hasidism opposed the externalization of the Maggid's preaching and the idolatry of the Talmudist's learning. It attacked the inclemency of intellectuality, the rigidity of legalism, a system of life that had become chilly. The Hasid studied the Talmud also to experience its soul, to envision worlds. Hasidism brought warmth, light, enthusiasm; it set life aflame. It was one of the great conquests of Jewish history. The admonition not to fool others was given a new turn: don't fool yourself. Truthfulness, wholeheartedness, was central. The aphorism became a mode for Hasidic thinking. The parable took on new power. Doctrines affected life and were transformed into attitudes and facts. Hasidism learned how to fight with the enemies' weapons—the evil urge (*yetzer hara'*) and joy (*simḥah*). It taught that holiness was something concrete and positive. To redeem the sparks was earthly serving. There are two ways of instilling discipline: knowledge of the Law and understanding its meaning: Halakhah and Kabbalah. At a time when the spectacular phenomenon of *lamdanut* (Talmudic learning) was praised, Hasidism stressed *'anavah* (humility), the imponderable, the inaudible. It taught reverence, enthusiasm. It taught that scholarship for its own sake could be an idol, that God is greater than sin."[1]

"It was a time," Heschel adds, "when the Jewish imagination was nearly exhausted. The mind had reached an impasse, thinking about impossible possibilities in Talmudic law. The heart was troubled by oppressive social and eco-

nomic conditions, as well as the teachings of ascetic preach-
ers. Then a miracle occurred. It was as if Providence had
proclaimed, 'Let there be light!' And there was light—in the
form of an individual: Reb Israel, son of Eliezer, Baal Shem
Tov, 'Master of the Good Name.' . . .

"He was born in a small town in the province of Podolia,
Okop, to poor and elderly parents. Orphaned as a child, he
later eked out a living as an assistant teacher of small children.
Tradition has it that at the age of twenty he went into seclusion in the Carpathian Mountains for spiritual training and
preparation for his calling. There he lived for several years as
a digger of clay, which his wife sold in the local town where
she kept house. When he was thirty-six he revealed himself
as a spiritual master. Later he settled in Mezbizh . . . where
he died in 1760. . . .

"The Baal Shem Tov was the founder of the Hasidic
movement, and Mezbizh was the cradle in which a new understanding of Judaism was nurtured.

"When millions of our people were still alive in Eastern
Europe and their memory and faith vibrated with thought,
image, and emotion, the mere mention of Reb Israel Baal
Shem Tov cast a spell upon them. The moment one uttered
his name, one felt as if [one's] lips were blessed and [one's]
soul grew wings. . . .

"During his lifetime, Reb Israel inspired a large number
of disciples to follow him. After his death his influence became even more widespread. Within a generation, the insights he formulated at Mezbizh had captivated the Jewish
masses with new spiritual ideas and values. And Mezbizh became the symbol of Hasidism.

"Rarely in Jewish history has one man succeeded in up-
lifting so many individuals to a level of greatness. . . . No
one in the long chain of charismatic figures that followed
him was equal to the Baal Shem.

"Hasidism represents an enigma. It is first of all the enigma
of the impact of one great man, the Besht [acronym for Baal
Shem Tov], . . . who in a very short time was able to capture
the majority of the Jewish people and to keep them under

his spell for generations. What was there about him that was not to be found in other great Jewish personalities like Maimonides or even Isaac Luria or Akiba? . . . The answers given are partly sociological, partly historical; I believe there is also a Hasidic answer to this Hasidic riddle."

Heschel explains that in the royal succession in Poland in those days (the eighteenth century) two unusual conditions prevailed: one did not become king by birth but was elected by noblemen, and even non-Poles could be candidates. So, when the king died and there would be an election, princes from faraway lands competed by sending their representatives. Each representative claimed that his candidate was the wisest, the wealthiest, the ablest. This went on for days. No decision was reached, until one noble actually brought his candidate to the people, saying: "Here, see how grand he is!" That man was elected.

"Many Jews talked about God," Heschel continued, "but it was the Besht who brought God to the people. This is perhaps the best answer to the question of how to explain the unbelievable impact of this great man in such a short time.

Reb Israel Baal Shem Tov "revealed the Divine as present even in our shabby world, in every little thing, and especially in man. He made us realize that there was nothing in man— neither limb nor movement—that did not serve as vessel or vehicle for the Divine force. No place was devoid of the Divine. He taught that the Zaddikim who grasped the bond between Creator and creature were blessed with so great a power that they were able to perform marvelous acts of mystical unification in the sphere of the Divine. Furthermore, every man in this world could work deeds that might affect the worlds above. Most important, attachment to God was possible, even while we are carrying out mundane tasks or making small talk. Thus, unlike the sages of the past, who delivered discourses about God, the Baal Shem, like the wise man in the parable, brought God to every man. . . .

"The Baal Shem brought about a radical shift in the religious outlook of Jewry. In ancient times the sanctuary in Jeru-

salem had been the holy center from which expiation and
blessing radiated out to the world. But the sanctuary was in
ruins, the soul of Israel in mourning. Then the Baal Shem
established a new center: the Tzaddik, the Rebbe—he was
to be the sanctuary. For the Baal Shem believed that a man
could be the true dwelling place of the Divine. He brought
about the renewal of man in Judaism.

"The Jewish people is not the same since the days of the
Besht. It is a new people. Other personalities contributed
great works; they left behind impressive achievements; the
Besht left behind a new people. To many Jews the mere
fulfillment of regulations was the essence of Jewish living.
. . . The Besht taught that Jewish life is an occasion for exaltation. Observance of the Law is the basis, but exaltation
through observance is the goal. . . . Other great teachers
bore the message of God, sang His praises, lectured about
His attributes and wondrous deeds. The Baal Shem brought
not only the message; he brought God Himself to the people. His contribution, therefore, consisted of more than illu-
mination, insights, and ideas; he helped mold into being new
types of personality: the Hasid and the Tzaddik. . . . [T]he
greatness of the Besht was that he was the beginning of a
long series of . . . moments of inspiration. And he holds us
in his spell to this very day. He who really wants to be up-
lifted by communing with a great person whom he can love
without reservation, who can enrich his thought and imagination without end, that person can meditate about the life
. . . of the Besht. There has been no one like him during the
last thousand years."[2]

From the unique as well as fascinating analysis in the above
paragraphs, it is understandable why many claim that, although he was a master of many fields of study, in none is
the loss of Abraham Joshua Heschel felt more keenly than
that of Hasidism. A growing number of students have begun
to take seriously Martin Buber's long-denied claim that Hasidism was the most significant phenomenon in the history
of religion during the past two and a half centuries. The new
academic and popular interest in Hasidism has sparked a

plethora of works on the subject in Hebrew and English, and a growing number of courses are being offered in institutions of higher learning. While the "decline" of the Hasidic movement has received generous attention from scholars, the evidence of its communal and intellectual vitality is only now beginning to receive a hearing. If it is not on the same exalted level as it was in its first three generations, the movement has nevertheless continued with unabated vigor, regularly producing a formidable series of leaders and a constantly growing, if uneven, literature. Despite early separatist tendencies, Hasidism returned to (and was admitted by) the official Jewish community, while in the second half of the twentieth century—even after the Holocaust—it has shown itself capable of taking root in the democratic societies of the West. Consider, for example, the fact that a disproportionate number of Jews who have made signal contributions to contemporary culture—Agnon in literature, Chagall in art, and Buber and Heschel in philosophy—emerged from a Hasidic milieu. All this, if touched on by publicists, has by and large been ignored by scholars.[3] Heschel, whose studies on Maimonides and Abravanel demonstrated his understanding of the Spanish epoch, argued that the "golden period" of Jewish history was not in Spain but in Eastern Europe. For him the acme of Eastern European Jewry was Hasidism, the high point of post-Talmudic Jewish history.

While Heschel's specifically Hasidic studies are confined to the essays in *The Circle of the Baal Shem Tov*, and to the monumental work on Rabbi Menahem Mendel of Kotzk, his other writings often reflect Hasidic sources and insights. Indeed, the more familiar one becomes with Hasidic literature, the more one understands how Heschel drew upon these sources. The influence of Hasidism is reflected in Heschel's contributions to the understanding of the phenomenology of prophecy and of *ruah hakodesh* (the holy spirit). There are, for example, clear echoes of Hasidic concepts and concerns in Heschel's excursions upon the Sabbath as a bride, upon "divine pathos," the "ineffable," "radical amazement," the illusion of God's absence, the "holy dimension" of all reality, the "primacy of inwardness," the criticism of "panhalachism," the centrality of prayer, the "dignity of words," and the "endless yearning." Some of the section headings in *Man Is Not Alone* might, in fact, be transposed to a book on Hasidic philosophy. In the final chapter of his work on Maimonides, where he described the great philosopher's last years when he abandoned his scholarly undertakings for a life of *imitatio Dei,* one catches a reflection of the zaddik for whom "living" Torah is more important than "writing" Torah.[4]

The State of Hasidic Research

To understand Heschel as a scholar of Hasidism, it would be helpful to review the general state of Hasidic research. One might describe it as both problematic and promising.

Hasidic research is problematic, because so little was done in the past that was of lasting value and upon which one could build. Anti-Hasidic prejudice in the West kept many students from contributing to the field and rendered the work of others ineffective. With the absence, until recently, of university-level courses in Hasidism and professorships, fellowships, or research grants, few were encouraged to enter a field with so bleak a future. Earlier studies can be characterized either by over-enthusiasm or by lack of sensitivity. Hasidism was either romanticized or maligned. The absence of a balanced approach to the subject has been a major obstacle. New movements are bound to engender advocates and critics. Hasidism, because of its nature and its claims, aroused a storm of controversy. Fervor characterized both its proponents and its enemies. Attack was followed by counterattack, forgery by counter-forgery. The burning of books, excommunications, and courting the interference of government authorities were the order of the day. In time, though matters quieted down—partly because the Hasidic movement had grown so powerful that it had to be received back into the community—much of the literature remained impas-

sioned, extreme, and bitter. As a result, the contemporary
scholar has at his disposal a minimum of evenhanded and
well-informed studies congruent with Hasidism's depth and
breadth. In 1952 Heschel observed that

> in the field of Jewish scholarship there are few subjects about
> which so much has been written in so dilettantish a manner
> as the history of Hasidism. Few researchers have followed the
> fine example set by Eliezer Tzvi Hakohen Zweifel with his
> work *Shalom 'al Yisra'el* (Zhitomir, 1868–69). . . . Samuel
> Abba Horodezky's important monographs did not concern
> themselves sufficiently with details. Dubnow, in his notewor-
> thy *History of Hasidism*, paid more attention to the opponents
> of Hasidism, the Mitnagdim, than to Hasidism itself. . . .[5]

The lack of surviving documents is a second obstacle to a
proper understanding of the movement. Referring to the
post-Holocaust situation, Heschel noted in the same article
that "we remain unsure of thousands of simple facts: bio-
graphical dates, bibliographic details, identification of names,
etc. This sorry state of affairs is due in part to the fact that
research on Hasidism suffers from a dearth of documents."[6]
Although Heschel was writing about the post-Holocaust
condition, such a vacuum had, in fact, long prevailed in the
great Jewish libraries of Western Europe and America, upon
which most historical research on Judaism was dependent.
The author of the major work on Shabbetai Tzvi observed
to me that it was easier to write a study on that subject than
on some noted Hasidic figure, for while Sabbatean manuscripts were being avidly collected by the Jewish librarians
of the West, who considered them bizarre testimony of a
movement long dead, Hasidic documents, even the most
valuable, though readily accessible—Hasidism, after all, was
a living, challenging phenomenon—were virtually ignored
as worthless.[7] The librarians followed the example of their
doyen, Moritz Steinschneider, the master bibliographer who
insatiably ransacked every nook and cranny in search of Hebrew manuscripts, but freely admitted that he knew next
to nothing about Hasidic literature. Sabbateanism, though

heretical, was after all a curiosity, while Hasidism was a contemporary calamity, a "malady of Judaism."[8]

A case in point is Elkan Adler, the noted English barrister,
book collector, and son of the former chief rabbi. While his
anti-Hasidism seems a somewhat gentler British version, it
no doubt played a role in what he felt was of value to collect.
The description he gives in his travel book of "Hasidic" joy
on Simḥat Torah around the turn of the century in Jerusalem
includes seeing himself as

> Gulliver among the Brobdingnagians, when the monkeys pa-
> tronized him. . . . If the tune of the Chassidim is funny . . . a
> Chassidish howl, . . . [and] the harmonization rather like a
> Chassid's nightmare after a heavy supper of Beethoven! . . .
> the manner in which they make the Hakafoth, or circuits of
> the Synagogue, during the Rejoicing of the law, is funnier
> still. It was comical and shocking to see venerable gray beards
> pirouetting on their toes like some European fairy of the pan-
> tomime, but it was highly appreciated, and I had to simulate
> satisfaction for fear of being rebuked, as Michal was when she
> objected to King David's "dancing with all his might."[9]

An unusual combination of Jewish knowledge and aristo-
cratic wealth, Adler literally scoured the earth in search of
rare Hebrew books. He managed to collect manuscripts at
the rate of about one hundred a year and to visit each of the
continents, except Australia, half a dozen times or so in
search of them.[10] Yet the important catalogue of his manuscripts, which represents a significant part of the collection
of its present owner, the library of the Jewish Theological
Seminary of America, reveals hardly a single Hasidic work.

Another problem in Hasidic research is the separation, by
predilection or circumstance, between some Hasidic scholarship and familiarity with Hasidic life. In other disciplines,
such disjuncture may not have serious consequences. The
essence of Hasidism, however, was the living reality of
which the written word, impressive and vast as it is, is often
not an adequate reflection. Hasidism was more than the philosophy that could be distilled from its classics. It was a cer-

tain style of life. With the demise of Eastern European Jewry, the living tradition was severely attenuated. Heschel writes:

> Whoever attempts to describe Hasidism on the basis of literary sources alone without drawing upon the oral tradition ignores the authentic living source and is dependent upon material artificial in character. In the absence of the oral tradition and a proximity to Hasidic personages, one can scarcely describe Hasidism. Its essence was rarely expressed in writing, and what was written down was translated into Hebrew in a style that seldom captured the living tongue of the masters.
>
> Hasidic literature is a literature of translation, and not always successful translation. In order to understand Hasidism one must learn how to listen and how to stand close to those who lived it.[11]

And again:

> [It] is a tragedy that this great movement is essentially an oral movement, one that cannot be preserved in written form. It is ultimately a living movement. It is not contained fully in any of its books. . . . [In] other words, Hasidism has a very personal dimension. . . . To be a Hasid is to be in love with God and with what God has created. Once you are in love you are a different human being. . . . That is the history of Hasidism. Indeed, he who has never been in love will not understand and may consider it a madness. That is why there is so much opposition to Hasidism, more than we are willing to admit.[12]

Some modern scholars, not familiar or sympathetic with Hasidic life, may be limited almost exclusively to its literature and by necessity approach their subject like astronomers, biologists, . . . or tourists.

Hasidic literature itself, finally, is intrinsically difficult to penetrate. It is enigmatic, terse, usually the work of a disciple transcribing the words of his master, often written in a poor Hebrew that is nothing more than a translation of the original spoken Yiddish,[13] characterized by allusions to kabbalistic formulae, and presupposing a knowledge of the rabbinical texts. The writings of Hasidism, though filled with brilliant

insights and profound exposition, present a formidable obstacle to the student. One need only observe that although
Hasidic literature numbers about three thousand items, we
lack a bibliography, an adequate study of its nature and extent, a comprehensive, quality anthology, and a critical edition of and commentary to even a handful of its classic
texts.[14]

In a little-known article,[15] Heschel once suggested that the
attitude toward Hasidism of the *Wissenschaft* scholars of the
West was yet another example of their wholesale rejection
of the Ashkenazic tradition in favor of the supposedly more
liberal, "cultured," and decorous Sephardic mode. To demonstrate his point, he included one of his rare references to
contemporary writers:

> In the modern period, its [the Sephardic] influence permeated
> other Jewish groups, especially in Germany. It was the admi-
> ration of the 19th-century German Jewish scholars for the
> Sephardic Middle Ages that determined the mood of the
> modern "Science of Judaism" (*Wissenschaft des Judentums*).
>
> The scholars of emancipated German Jewry saw in the
> Spanish period the "Golden Age" of Jewish history, and cele-
> brated it as a happy blend of progress and traditionalism upon
> which they desired to model their own course. In their re-
> search they went to the point of applying the cultural stan-
> dards of the "Golden Age" to the literature of later centuries.
> For some Jewish scholars, any Jewish literature dating after
> 1492, the year in which Jewish life in Spain ceased, was not
> considered worthy of scholarly investigation. Their example
> was followed in forming the curricula of the higher schools
> of Jewish learning, which gave no place to works written after
> 1492 and before the beginning of modern Hebrew literature.
>
> This desire for inner identification with the Spanish Jewish
> period reflected itself in the synagogue architecture of the
> 19th century. Liberal Jewish synagogues in Central Europe
> were built in the Moorish style as if the stucco arabesque,
> horseshoe arches, and dados of glazed and painted tiles were
> the aptest possible expressions of the liberal Jew's religious
> mood.
>
> Hand in hand with the romantic admiration of the Sephar-

dim that became one of the motifs of Reform Judaism in
Germany went social aspirations, too. The social standing of
the few Sephardim in Germany was superior to that of the
Ashkenazim, and the leaders of the new Reform movement,
anxious to develop a new and more advanced way of Jewish
life that would abandon the traditional forms still adhered to
by the Jewish masses, often blatantly imitated the manners of
the Sephardim. In the Portuguese synagogues they found that
solemnity and decorum which they missed in the old *shul*. It
was hardly for scientific reasons that the Sephardic pronuncia-
tion of Hebrew was introduced in the early "temples." . . .

[T]he modern Ashkenazic Jew, particularly in Central Europe, often came to lose his appreciation of the value of his
own original way of life. He developed an embarrassed aversion for the dramatic, for the moving and vivid style, whether
in the synagogue or in human relations. For him dignity grew
to mean something to be achieved by strict adherence to an
established, well-balanced, mannerly form undisturbed by any
eruption of the sudden and spontaneous. Thus Hermann
Cohen wrote in 1916 that the elimination of the dramatic
manner from the worship of East European Jews would turn
the synagogues into "seats of true culture."

This lack of understanding for and alienation from the values of the Ashkenazic traditions became complete. Describing
the way in which the Hasidim prayed, a prominent Jewish
historian, in a work first published in 1913 and reprinted in
1931, could write:

"The [Hasidic] movement did not signify a gain for religious life; the asset that lay in its striving for inwardness was
more than cancelled out by the preposterousness of its superstitious notions and of its unruly behavior. . . . According to
its principles, Hasidism meant a total revolt against the divine
service [sic!]; nothing could have made the untenability of the
latter more striking than the fact that great numbers of people
should turn away from it, not out of scepticism or doubt,
but out of a most intense yearning for piety. . . . Hasidism
contributed to the deterioration rather than to the improve-
ment of the divine service. . . . its noise and wild, restless
movements brought new factors of disturbance. . . . It is no
wonder that at such a time complaints were made about the
lack of devoutness and attention, about the disorder and inter-

ruptions. The divine service stood in need of a thorough renovation and restoration if it was to survive. The modern age [read: the Reform movement —A.J.H.] supplied both."

The book Heschel referred to is *Der jüdische Gottesdienst*, the standard work on Jewish liturgy, by Ismar Elbogen, his former teacher at the Liberal rabbinical school in Berlin and one of the leading figures in *die Wissenschaft des Judentums* (the movement for the scientific study of Judaism).[16] Other expressions of this point of view have not been uncommon. For example, according to the system of organization of one of the standard library catalogues for Judaica, "Hasidism" is listed under the rubric "sects," along with the Essenes, the Karaites, and the Samaritans.[17] As early as 1887, perhaps the most distinguished figure associated with the development of American Jewish scholarship, Solomon Schechter, published a sympathetic article on Hasidism in English ("The Chassidim," first read before the Jews College Literary Society, November 13, 1887, later printed in the *Jewish Chronicle*, and reprinted in his *Studies in Judaism*).[18] Virtually none on this continent were to emulate him. Among the more than seventy volumes of the *Jewish Quarterly Review*, the more than forty volumes of the *Proceedings of the American Academy for Jewish Research*, and the more than fifty volumes of the *Hebrew Union College Annual*, only a handful of articles relating to Hasidism have appeared—and these, more often, to anti-Hasidism![19] It would be fair to conclude that the approach to Hasidism of *die Wissenschaft des Judentums* was perpetuated, until most recently, by its American advocates.

But if the state of Hasidic scholarship is problematic, it is also promising. Much has occurred since Heschel made his critical observations. In both Israel and the Diaspora, an entire battery of scholars, too many to name, have emerged, producing a veritable barrage of books and studies, some of great value, including the tracing of kabbalistic origins, philosophical analyses, and historical studies such as the unearthing of Polish documents of the time. The flood of new scholarship stems primarily from the school of Gershom

Scholem and reflects both the insights and the limitations of its mentor.

Several reasons might be suggested for this elevated interest in Hasidism. One reason is spiritual. It has to do with what Daniel Bell has called the "exhaustion of modernity," that is, the failure first of technology and then of "culture" (literature–art–music) as substitutes for religion. After several centuries in which "natural" man has explored the secular kingdom in a failed search for redemption, there has been unlocked a receptivity to the sacred dimension of reality, accounting, in some measure, for the new attentiveness to the Hasidic movement. A second reason is historical. The catastrophic end of a thousand years of Eastern European Jewish communal life has stimulated considerable effort to document and understand what was previously taken for granted and, consequently, in good measure, overlooked. Studies on Hasidism, formerly so scant, are today considered of sufficient interest to warrant their publication in major scholarly journals.

Formerly, no courses in Hasidism had been offered at American institutions of higher learning, even Jewish institutions; today, the number rises each year, as does the number of doctoral dissertations on or related to Hasidism. One noteworthy early product of the new research was the publication of the first critical edition of a classic Hasidic work with full commentary.[20] Out-of-print volumes have been photocopied, or newly set, some with helpful indices. Whole batteries of books have appeared, both scientific and pietistic, while research into Hasidism has become so formidable an undertaking that staid academies dare not ignore it. Scholarship of every stripe endeavors to plumb its depths and sift the ashes. Hasidic study has become a veritable industry. Still we do not have a reliable history of the movement or an introduction to its ideas.

Heschel's warnings remain. Most documents have vanished forever. The oral tradition is no longer verifiable. And the authentic living reality of Hasidism is questionable. Though Hasidism itself is remarkably vital, the Holocaust experience has driven Hasidism to an extremism which early became a feature of the movement, serving to further obscure its former greatness. One strains to find in post-Holocaust Hasidism either the Besht's heart or the Kotzker's head; it exhibits less of the spirit of Levi Yitzhak (known for his love for all Israel) and more of Satmar (Rabbi Joel Teitelbaum, d. 1979, known for his narrow zealotry). Finally, the stress upon magic, mysticism, and gender, while legitimate subjects for inquiry, minimizes what Heschel considered the essence of the movement: its social and communal reality, its style of life. Heschel's belief that Hasidism was the most vital aspect of modern Judaism—part of what he called "the golden period of Jewish history"[21]—as well as his conviction that Hasidism must play a central role for any renewal of Judaism today, have proved substantially correct.

Buber and Scholem

Among the few scholars of the West who repudiated the outlook of *jüdische Wissenschaft* and contributed to a reawakening of interest in Hasidism were Martin Buber and Gershom Scholem. Their motives were only partly the same.

Buber opposed *jüdische Wissenschaft's* stress on rationalism, philology, and positivism and its pursuit of a historiography "which sees the past as a meaningless 'promiscuous agglomeration of happenings,'" thus fragmenting "Jewish history into many tiny problems."[22] Scholem understood *jüdische Wissenschaft* as the "academic mortician" of Judaism. Referring to the polemical purposes of the Western scholars who, in the throes of emancipation, were embarrassed by and sought to dismiss the unpleasant evidence of mysticism in Judaism, he wrote:

> Factors that have been emphasized and were considered positive from the world-view of assimilation and self-justification now require an entirely new analysis in order to determine what their actual role was in the development of the nation. Factors that were denigrated will appear in a different, more

positive light from this point of view. . . . It is possible that
what was termed degeneracy will be thought of as a revelation
and light and what seemed to [nineteenth-century historians]
will be revealed as a great living myth . . . not the washing
and mummification of the dead, but the discovery of hidden
life by removal of the obfuscating masks.[23]

Although both Buber and Scholem were agreed in their rejection of the apologetic-rationalist-philological approach of
die Wissenschaft des Jüdentums, the two were to follow different directions in their work. A reading of their controversy
on the proper post-*Wissenschaft* approach to Hasidism is of
considerable interest; for my purposes, moreover, the two
approaches help to provide a context within which to view
the contributions of Abraham Joshua Heschel.[24]

Toward the beginning of the century, Buber, through his
lyric German rendition of the Hasidic tale, brought the startling message of Hasidism to the Western Jew and to the
gentile. He was only the best-known figure of the neo-Hasidic
revival which included such writers as Berdichevsky, Peretz,
Horodetzky, and Y. Steinberg, most of whom were national-
ists or members of the intelligentsia, rebelling against the traditional pattern of Jewish study.

Gershom Scholem and his school repudiated not only *jüdische Wissenschaft* but neo-Hasidism as well, particularly Martin Buber's understanding of Hasidism. They pointed to his
preference for Hasidic legend over the discursive writings as
well as his penchant for exposition which emphasized mysticism or existential "decision" at the expense of the real
meaning of the text and the centrality of tradition. Though
Scholem would not have gone as far as Hurwitz, who attacked neo-Hasidism for "searching for pearls in piles of gar-
bage," he did adopt almost all of Hurwitz's "critique of
Hasidism as a quietistic movement" and of Sabbateanism as
a model of historical vitality.[25] He acknowledged Buber's
contribution as a groundbreaking effort, but argued that it
glossed over the less attractive aspects of Hasidism and was
self-serving and overly selective in its emphasis. As Buber's
general thinking moved from mysticism to existentialism, so

did his understanding of Hasidism. Thus, during the first phase, before World War I, he dealt with the "ecstatic quality" of Hasidism. Later, he emphasized Hasidism's "hallowing of the everyday" and its concern for the "concrete here and now."
The approach of the dominant Scholem school is no less problematic. Scholem credited the period of Shabbetai Tzvi as the watershed of modern Jewish history. He viewed the false messiah as a liberator who broke the millennial rabbinic hegemony and thereby facilitated, in greater or lesser measure, the emergence of such movements as Haskalah, Zionism, Reform, and Hasidism. For Scholem, "pluralism" replaced "normative" as the key word in the new Jewish historiography, providing, alongside Halakhah and philosophy, a place for mysticism, and even such undercurrents as antinomianism.[26]
While contributing significantly to the understanding of the Hasidic text, both as to its historical authenticity and as to its relation to the older Kabbalah, the Scholem school betrays at times its own selective weakness for the gnostic, the quietistic, and the supposedly Sabbatean elements in the literature of Hasidism. Critics have made their points. R. J. Z. Werblowsky sees Scholem's attempt to raise Sabbateanism to the level of rabbinic Judaism as a dangerous misreading of Jewish history; Kurzweil questions Scholem's historical objectivity in view of the latter's anarchical emphasis on the irrational in contrast to the halakhic and rational elements in Judaism; Jacob Katz is doubtful whether historical sources support a causal relationship between Sabbateanism and modern Jewish movements;[27] while M. Piekarz argues that numerous Hasidic statements, which Scholem traces to Sabbatean texts, merely share a common source in earlier classic Musar works such as *Sheney Luḥot Ḥabrit* and *Re'shit Hokhmah*.[28]
Die Wissenschaft des Judentums, because of its stress on polemics and rationalism, either ignored or demeaned Hasidism. Buber, the foremost representative of the neo-Hasidic revival, while cultivating the tale and showing the contem-

porary relevance of several of the central Hasidic themes, can
be faulted for often interpreting Hasidism in terms of his
personal philosophy, whether mystical or existential. Scholem, who opened modern Jewish historiography to the dimension of the mystical and the mythical, tended to
overlook the moral and the enduring religious message of
Hasidism, by virtue of his concentration on the kabbalistic
and the Sabbatean, as well as his distance from Hasidic life
itself.

Both Buber and Scholem rejected Jewish tradition as a
pattern for their personal lives, and both pursued theories
that support their own positions. Buber's central emphasis
on Hasidism was upon the existential decision. (A favorite
tale of his is about the master who asked his disciples, "What
is the most important thing in the world?" One answers,
"the Sabbath"; another "prayer"; a third, "Yom Kippur."
"No," the master explains, "the most important thing is
whatever you are doing at the moment!") Neither was familiar with authentic Hasidic life.

> Buber as a religious anarchist rejected the notion of an au-
> thoritative revelation and historical tradition. Out of hostility
> toward both orthodox halakhic Judaism and rational Jewish
> philosophy, Buber rejected the burden of tradition and cre-
> ated his counterhistory by a subjective, mythopoeic "act of
> decision."[29] Scholem also labels himself a religious anarchist,
> but . . . he means something quite different from Buber.
> Scholem . . . argued that Judaism actually consists of an anar-
> chistic plurality of sources. . . . When Scholem calls himself a
> religious anarchist, he means that the historical tradition,
> which is the only source of knowledge we have of revelation,
> contains no one authoritative voice. All that can be learned
> from the study of history is the *struggle* for absolute values
> among conflicting voices of authority. Scholem is an anarchist
> because he believes "the binding character of the Revelation
> for a collective has disappeared. The word of God no longer
> serves as a source for the definition of possible contents of a
> religious tradition and thus of a possible theology."[30]

Both Buber's emphasis on mysticism and/or existential decision in Hasidism and Scholem's search for Sabbatean influences reflect antinomian sympathies.

Heschel as a Scholar of Hasidism

For Heschel, Hasidism was not romanticism, not rebellion, not an affirmation of Orthodoxy. He could not be labeled a neo-Hasid, though he forsook the Hasidic enclave for the broader Western society; nor did he find Hasidism shot through with Sabbatean elements, though he was well aware of the origins and history of the movement. Indeed, in his understanding of Hasidism, Heschel had no peer. His grasp of the entire range of Jewish literature—biblical, rabbinic, philosophic, and mystical—enabled him to discern in what sense Hasidic writings were a continuation of or a departure from the past, where they were original, what elements of earlier Jewish thought they accepted or rejected, and what problems they attempted to address. Philosophically, he was able to place Hasidism within a wider spiritual context; historically, he sought to gather those bits of evidence that, properly evaluated and pieced together, might reveal a hitherto unknown aspect of a personality or an event. Heschel's mastery of Hasidic texts themselves was such that, when works were cited during discussions, he usually had no need to see the printed volume to quote from it extensively. Heschel's control of the material was joined by highly disciplined study habits.

An example of his phenomenal memory is apropos. A most rare Hasidic book once came into my possession. Delighted, I was off the next morning to show it to the leading dealer in Hasidic books, who promptly offered me a goodly sum for it; from there I went to the principal Hasidic bibliographer, who wanted to photocopy it; late in the afternoon I arrived with my treasure at Heschel's study. He told me to sit down, read the small volume in about twenty minutes, and returned it to me. None of the three had ever seen the book before: one wanted to buy it, another wanted to copy it; Heschel simply memorized it!

Despite the fact that Hasidic literature is characterized by considerable shortcomings, which I have already alluded to, the effect of the publication and dissemination of the early

Hasidic writings was like a series of thunderbolts that shat-
tered as well as enlightened. Of those who read these trea-
tises, few remained unmoved, some becoming angry critics
of the new movement, others fervent followers. So avidly
did the devotees pore over these books in the years that followed that they virtually devoured them, and soon a first
edition in good condition could hardly be found. Hasidic
literature was, and was meant to be, evocative as well as cognitive, addressing the soul and the mind at once. The
"word," so central to the entire Hasidic enterprise, was, in
its written form, says Heschel, "a voice, not a mere idea."
To him, whose approach to Hasidism was never that of pure
research, the task of the present student of this literature becomes, therefore, "how to hear the voice through the
words." Heschel's trenchant observations are contained in
his preface to my study of Rabbi Jacob Joseph of Polonnoye,
author of the first and, in some ways, still the most significant
Hasidic book:

> The Holy of Holies in the Temple at Jerusalem was a place
> which only the High Priest was allowed to enter once a year,
> on the Day of Atonement. Now, even the Holy of Holies was
> occasionally in need of repair. To provide for such an occa-
> sion, there were openings in the Upper Chamber leading
> [down] through the ceiling of the Holy of Holies and close
> to its walls. Through these openings they used to lower the
> workmen in boxes (*Tevot*), which were open only to the
> walls, "so that they should not feast their eyes on the Holy of
> Holies.
>
> It is said that the Upper Chamber of the Holy of Holies
> was even less accessible than the Holy of Holies, for the High
> Priest entered the Holy of Holies once a year, whereas the
> Upper Chamber was entered only once in fifty years to see
> whether any repairs were required.
>
> The great Hasidim were the repair men of the Holy of
> Holies. In Hebrew *tevot* means both boxes and *words*. It was
> through the word that they entered the Holy of Holies. In
> the Hasidic movement the spirit was alive in the word. It was
> a voice, not a mere idea. It emanated in words that had the
> power to repair, to revive, to create.

Judaism today is in need of repair. The spirit is stifled, the word is emaciated; we do not know how to find access to the "Upper Chamber."

Hasidism withers when placed on exhibition. Its substance is not perceptible to the eye. It is not enough to read its written word; one must hear it, one must learn to be perceptive to the voice. Fortunately there are words in many of its records which still ring with the passion and enthusiasm of those who spoke them. The problem is how to hear the voice through the words.

Neither the Baal Shem nor most of his disciples have written down their utterances. One of the very few who did write was Rabbi Yaakov Yosef. The surprise, the joy, the refreshment which the publication of his books brought to the Jewish world are quite understandable to those who are acquainted with the spiritual atmosphere of the eighteenth century. It was like questioning the Ptolemaic theory in the time of Copernicus. These books offered a transvaluation of accepted values, a fresh vision of what is at stake in Jewish faith and existence, and a singular sensitivity for the divine. These are words that originated in Paradise, said one of his contemporaries. In other books one must read many pages until the presence of God is sensed; in the writings of Rabbi Yaakov Yosef, God's presence is felt on each page.[31]

Heschel's Hasidic understanding went beyond books. He was intimately familiar with Hasidism as a living phenomenon, was privy to the legacy of tradition handed down from several of the most eminent Hasidic dynasties because of his early upbringing and continued association, and had remarkable sensitivity to the core of Hasidic authenticity as it was transmitted from generation to generation. Without acquaintance with the oral tradition of the movement, and with Hasidism as a living phenomenon, Hasidic scholarship, in Heschel's opinion, faces a major obstacle, which the demise of East European Jewry only serves to emphasize. His published views on this central issue revolve around the preparation of his last major work, the powerful two-volume Yiddish study on Rabbi Menahem Mendl of Kotzk.

Why, in his waning years, Heschel determined to write his

one major Hasidic work on the later master of Kotzk rather than the movement's founder, the Baal Shem Tov, whose life and thought had occupied him for decades, Heschel never told us. Perhaps the formidable problems which the paucity of historical sources presented for a comprehensive work on the Baal Shem—the need to collect, collate, and interpret scattered hints and pieces of information to establish dates, names, and places, comparing different versions of manuscripts and/or early prints, as well as contending with numerous other conflicting theories which would have to be presented and refuted—constituted too wearying a project for the final years of his life. A book on the Kotzker rebbe, on the other hand, whose teachings he had grappled with since youth, partly internalized, partly rejected, but was always enthralled by, might almost write itself.

Whether or not this explanation as to the subject of his final major study satisfies our curiosity, there is a second problem about the language of the study that Heschel himself answers: namely, why he wrote his book on Kotzk in Yiddish. Surely, he knew that to do so was to limit severely the work's future readership and that either English or Hebrew would have been preferable from the point of view of the future use of the book. In his explanation that he resolved to use Yiddish as the language of the work in order to preserve the authentic legacy of Kotzk, a literary monument of the highest order, Heschel's understanding of the relationship between the oral tradition and Hasidic scholarship comes to the fore:

> The words of the Kotzker Rebbe have simmered within me all my life. Even when [I was] not in agreement, I felt their powerful thrust. Though my way has not been without hardship, when I thought of the Kotzker Rebbe everything difficult became easier. Rabbi Mendl occupied himself with problems that, though we may not always be aware of them, disturb us to this very day. The answers he proposed may be hard for modern man to accept, but his perception was revolutionary, his impact shattering. Whoever is for but an hour in the presence of the Kotzker will never again give way to smugness.

One of the qualities of the Kotzker Rebbe was a marvelous gift in formulating his thoughts in a tense, sharp, and brilliant manner. Reading those of his aphorisms that have been preserved in the distinctive manner in which they were uttered, that is, in Yiddish, reveals an extraordinary style and power. Unfortunately, those who published Rabbi Mendl's words translated them into Hebrew, for seldom in Jewish history has the talent for conversion into felicitous Hebrew been so lacking as among those learned Jewish circles in Poland of the last century. Consequently, a number of his sayings . . . are garbled. That I understand them despite their ambiguous Hebrew formulation is due to the fact that in my youth I heard many of these aphorisms in their original Yiddish. It was my good fortune to have known Rabbi Ben Tzion and Rabbi Moses Judah, who had visited Rabbi Mendl, as well as a large number of Hasidim who were thoroughly imbued with the way of the Kotzk. From them I learned many of the aphorisms which I cite in this book. . . .

Some oral statements have survived which are more correct than their literary form. While the oral tradition preserved what was spoken by the rabbis, the literary text conveys them only as they were translated into Hebrew. One who has been close to Hasidic life knows with what reverence the words of the Masters were transmitted after they were "heard." One literally lived with them, was nourished by them: every effort was taken to transmit such words accurately.

When he was surrounded by so many great scholars, why did none of them write down Rabbi Mendel's words, as students of other tzaddikim had? The Kotzker himself asked his disciple, Rabbi Yehiel Meir, to record his teachings, but he did not. In my opinion it was because of an unwillingness to do so in Yiddish. The words Rabbi Mendl spoke in Yiddish were not easily rendered into Hebrew. To translate them exactly was not possible, while to record them in Yiddish was not acceptable. Thus Kotzk remained an oral tradition. . . . What I have written in this book about the Kotzker, whether his personality or his way, reflects the tradition of Kotzker Hasidim. . . .[32]

It has been suggested that the low estimate in which Hasidism was formerly held in the scholarly circles within which

Heschel was attempting to establish himself may have encouraged him in his early years to omit all but the most necessary references to Hasidic material in support of his
theories. The tragic end of Eastern European Jewry, however, brought new affirmation for what it had produced.
This, together with the growing acceptance of Heschel's
own works, encouraged him to make more open use of Hasidic literature. It is of interest that Heschel's first book in
1933, *Der Shem Hameforash: Mentsh* (Man: The Ineffable
Name of God), a youthful volume of Yiddish poetry, was
not listed in the initial bibliography of his works, which appeared in 1959, but is present in the updated 1965 version.[33]

Heschel observed privately more than once that "after the
Holocaust, Jewish scholarship should be devoted to that
which advances Yiddishkeit." He was warning that in the
terribly weakened position in which Jews found themselves
then, with the demise of the great centers of Jewish authority
and guidance and with their very survival at stake, they dared
not expend their limited resources on hairsplitting studies or
concentrating on the exposure of the unseemly side of Jewish life. Heschel was speaking to a situation in which some
Jewish scholars were content to edit texts, collect footnotes,
and frown upon ideas, questioning, for instance, whether
there was such a thing as Jewish theology, while others explored the Jewish "underworld," dwelling upon forgeries
and heresies.[34] Heschel preferred to devote himself, in a series of seminal works, to delineating wide areas of Jewish
creativity—biblical, rabbinic, medieval, and Hasidic. Even
his popular survey of Eastern European Jewry, *The Earth Is
the Lord's*, which reflects the enduring values of a thousand
years of Ashkenazic Jewry, stands in marked contrast to others' explorations of the occasionally insipid, bizarre, and rib-
ald. If Heschel may be faulted, it is in his tendency toward
Hasidic apologetics and his preference to stay clear of the
ignoble and dark features that are inevitable in a world that
included millions. To limit Jewish research in any way, however praiseworthy the motive, may result in an incomplete
view of the subject. The reader and the student must submit

the final verdict as to the relative reliability of those who sought, for whatever reasons, to portray a different and often more negative picture than Heschel did.

EXPECTATIONS, MENTORS, AND THE WEST ⁕

From Heschel's childhood on, there were Hasidic leaders who looked to him as one with unique promise for renewing Hasidic life. That was not to be, at least not in the way that they had hoped. Descended from Hasidic royalty on both his father's and his mother's side, young Heschel had talents that were recognized early, and though he was only a child of nine at the time of his father's death, the Hasidim began to bring him *kevitlekh* (petitions) and treat him as their rebbe. "We thought," said the rebbe of Kopyczynce (Kopitchinitz), a cousin and brother-in-law, "that he would be the Levi Yitzhak of our generation and rekindle Hasidism." A byword after his departure was that "had Heschel become a rebbe, all the other rebbes would have lost their Hasidim."[35] While his education had always been directed with special care in the selection of his teachers, even more attention was now paid in view of his promise, and it was during this period of his life that the influence of the remarkable Kotzker Hasid, Reb Bezalel, his teacher from the age of nine to twelve and a half (described by Heschel's childhood friend, Yehiel Hofer, the writer), was most keenly felt.

But awareness of the worlds "outside" was stirring, and the young Heschel did not accede to the wishes of the Hasidim. His curiosity was too consuming to ignore what lay beyond the narrow borders of the Jewish society of piety and learning of his ancestors in which he had been raised. Hofer relates how, at the age of seven or eight, Heschel once surprised him by compiling a detailed catalogue of the bolts of cloth that were piled in high columns in Hofer's father's millinery store, giving such information as color, material, quantity, price, etc., as an example of how Heschel insisted on mastering whatever new phenomenon drew his attention. Heschel's interest in secular studies must have begun in his teens. His decision to leave Warsaw for Berlin, by way of Vilna, to gain a secular education was received with trepidation. His mother, an unusual woman, clever and strong, who maintained their *shtibl* (the Hasidic house of prayer) after her husband's death and appreciated her son's gifts, noticed, when he was about fifteen, that she no longer heard him chanting the Talmud from his room, for he was now engaged in learning Polish, and she inquired why. He told her of his plan, and she communicated her concerns to the family in Vienna and Warsaw. A meeting of the family in Vienna was called by the Tchortkover Rebbe,[36] which Heschel may have attended. His mother's brother, the Novominsker Rebbe of Warsaw, at whose table Heschel grew up and one of the most powerful influences upon his life, tried to dissuade him, and agreed only when he saw that it was to no avail. "You can go," he finally told Heschel, "but *only* you." It was on a Saturday night after the close of the Sabbath that, having changed his Shabbos hat for an ordinary weekday cap, and accompanied by his cousin, a son of the Novominsker Rabbi, Heschel left Warsaw.

Just before the young Heschel was to depart his ancestral home in Poland for the secular society of the West, an old Hasid came to bid him farewell. Following the admonition that one should take leave with a word of Torah, the Hasid quoted the Mishnah (Avot 5:8) that cites, as "one of the ten miracles of the Temple in Jerusalem," that, no matter what the provocation, "the holy flesh [of the sacrifice] never became polluted." Then he told how Rabbi Barukh of Miedzybórz (Mezbizh) explained the passage: "One of the most wondrous miracles was, indeed, *lo' hisriah besar kodesh mey'-olam,* which is to say, 'the holy flesh'—that is, the people Israel— did not become polluted—*mey'-olam—from the world.*' "

"Avraham," the old Hasid concluded, taking him by the shoulders, "remember the word of Rabbi Barukh. *Lo' hisriah besar kodesh mey'-olam.* You, Avraham, you holy flesh, do not become polluted from the world!"

The Novominsker Rebbe, mentioned above, is important

for another reason. One of Heschel's major contributions as a religious thinker was his analysis of piety. He was a phenomenologist. He held that discursive reason, while essential, was, alone, inadequate to penetrate the inner recesses of religion. This could better be achieved through a description of the religious phenomena themselves, which, much as the artist's canvas, would have the power to evoke another level of comprehension. In composing his definitive picture of Jewish piety, Heschel drew from the lives and writings of holy men of the past, as well as from his own personal experience, but equally important were those he had known in his youth. One whom he identified to me as his principal model was the rabbi of Minsk Mazowiesk (Novominsk).

Rabbi Alter (a name added for long life) Israel Simon (after his grandfather) Perlow (1874–1933) was Heschel's mother's twin. The Novominsker's grandfather was a son-in-law of Rabbi Shlomo Hayim of Kedainai (Kaidenov), in the line of Mordecai of Nezkhizhtsh and Shlomo of Karlin, in White Russia, situated between Minsk and Vilna. It was there that the family lived. The Lithuanian stress on the study of Talmud lent a special tone to their Hasidism and had its effect on the young Heschel, whose Talmudic prowess was remembered. The father of the Novominsker, Jacob (1847–1902), was advised to "bring his type of Hasidism to Poland," and settled in Minsk Mazowiesk (Novominsk), just outside of Warsaw, where he established the first Hasidic yeshivah and a large synagogue with an impressive *Hof* or court. The privations of World War I drove the Novominsker, Alter Shimon, who succeeded his father in 1902 (though he had been at the head of the yeshivah since its founding in 1896), to remove to Warsaw itself, where he remained. His principal published work was *Tif'eret 'Ish*. The Novominsker was an unusual tzaddik. Famed for his Talmudic learning and as a kabbalist, he was also well known for his piety, Torah, and love of Israel. He presided at the third Sabbath meal, the *Shalosh Seudos*, in a mood of ecstasy. Those who were present reported that his songs and words of Torah were wonderful to hear, while his gestures and his face were marvelous to behold. He helped to bring Heschel's father to Warsaw, found a suitable place for him, and after the latter's early death, acted as mentor to the family. Heschel's uncle liked to have the young Abraham sit at his right hand when he spoke before the Hasidim at the Sabbath table.[37] The Novominsker's life, Heschel observed

> was consistent with his thought. . . . He was a complete person. Not one minute of the day was allowed to pass without attempting to serve God with all his strength. He gave himself over to a tremendous task: the service of the Almighty at every moment with every act. An ordinary *Minḥah* [the afternoon service] was like Yom Kippur elsewhere, and on the Sabbath, as he put each morsel of food into his mouth, he would say, *Lekoved Shabbos Kodesh*, "[I eat this] in honor of the holy Sabbath." This latter custom was not practiced even by my father, while the Gerer Hasidim who were the majority in Poland and followed the austere teachings of Kotzk, opposed it as excessive expression of one's feelings.[38]

Heschel left Warsaw for Vilna to study and graduate from the secular Yiddish Real-Gymnasium there, joining, during his stay, a circle of Yiddish poets, later known as the famed Yung Vilno, which included writers such as Abraham Sutzkever and Hayim Grade, who recalled in what high regard the youthful Heschel had been held. Shlomo Beillis, a fellow-poet, a Communist who resided in the East after the war, described his impressions of Heschel: "with the deep eyes of a *talmid hakham*, he came from a world far different from mine." When they took walks through the forest, Heschel "would surprise me by bringing along his dark hat and, upon entering the woods, would put it on. When I inquired for the reason, he replied in his soft voice: 'I don't know if you will understand. To me a forest is a holy place, and a Jew does not enter a holy place without covering his head. . . . The swaying trees are praying *shimen esre*.' "[39]

From Vilna Heschel moved west, to the University of Berlin and the Hochschule für die Wissenschaft des Judentums, to the Frankfurt Lehrhaus, and, after an eight-month return to Warsaw, on to England, and, finally, to America.

Contact with Western culture, particularly with German Jewry, its synagogues and academies of higher Jewish learning, made Heschel all the more certain that Hasidic thinking and living contained a treasure that should be made available to the emancipated Jew. His early studies on prophecy and Maimonides had stressed themes such as the divine pathos, the striving for prophecy, and *imitatio Dei*, concepts to which he had been sensitized by Hasidism. But what of Hasidism itself? What of that immense repository of surprising beauty and startling wisdom of which the West was not only ignorant but contemptuously ignorant? Where should one begin? Hasidism constituted a panorama of hundreds of remarkable spiritual figures, each with his own special way, and a literature whose books were precious, because, according to Rabbi Pinhas of Korzec, unlike other works, one did not have to turn countless pages in them to find God. Before understanding the contributions of its notable leaders and the meaning of its most important books, it was necessary to address the phenomenon of the Hasidic movement's creator, the Baal Shem Tov. This was the task to which Heschel began to direct himself.

The Baal Shem Tov

Perhaps the single most important project that Heschel left unfinished at his untimely death, a project for which he was uniquely suited and the completion of which students and scholars of Judaism had long awaited, was his work on the life and thought of the Baal Shem Tov, the renowned eighteenth-century founder of the Hasidic movement.[40] We do not know when Heschel first made plans to write this comprehensive work, but while he was in Cincinnati (1940–1945) he was already methodically gathering material. Perhaps the destruction of Hasidic life in Eastern Europe made him turn from those areas of Jewish thought in which he had been engaged, primarily the Bible and medieval philosophy, to a study of the movement he considered to be, in some ways, the final flowering of post-biblical Jewish history. Heschel's silent agony over the Holocaust during his years in Cincinnati (he rarely shared his pain with me, though I saw him several times a week from 1942 to 1944), as he failed in desperate attempts to influence public policy directly, led to his now classic portrait of Ashkenazic Jewry, in which he sketched its lasting qualities.[41]

Whatever the reasons, Heschel's book on the Besht was never written. Other works and projects, coming in quick succession, always postponed the book that must have been dearest to his heart. The closest he came were his remarks on the Besht in his investigation of Rabbi Menahem Mendel of Kotzk, which was finished at the very end of his life, as if at least one major statement on Hasidism had to be made before death snatched him away. In that book, a part of which he adapted into English as *A Passion for Truth* he dealt, as well, with the Besht. True, his purpose was to contrast the way of the Besht with that of Kotzk, the main subject of the work, but in his remarks on the Besht he condensed a number of valuable insights into the founder of Hasidism, allowing himself a personal statement (part of which was cited in the previous chapter on his life; here the focus is upon the Besht):

> I was born in Warsaw, Poland, but my cradle stood in Mezbizh (a small town in the province of Podolia, Ukraine), where the Baal Shem Tov, founder of the Hasidic movement, lived during the last twenty years of his life. That is where my father came from, and he continued to regard it as his home. . . . The earliest fascination I can recall is associated with the Baal Shem, whose parables disclosed some of the first insights I gained as a child. He remained a model too sublime to follow yet too overwhelming to ignore. . . .
>
> Years later I realized that, in being guided by both the Baal Shem Tov and the Kotzker, I had allowed two forces to carry on a struggle within me. One was occasionally mightier than the other. But who was to prevail, which was to be my guide? Both spoke convincingly, and each proved right on one level yet questionable on another.
>
> In a very strange way, I found my soul at home with the

Baal Shem but driven by the Kotzker. Was it good to live with one's heart torn between the joy of Mezbizh and the anxiety of Kotzk? . . . I had no choice: my heart was in Mezbizh, my mind in Kotzk.

I was taught about inexhaustible mines of meaning by the Baal Shem; from the Kotzker I learned to detect immense mountains of absurdity standing in the way. The one taught me song, the other—silence. The one reminded me that there could be a Heaven on earth, the other shocked me into discovering Hell in the alleged Heavenly places in our world.

The Baal Shem made dark hours luminous; the Kotzker eased wretchedness and desolation by forewarnings, by premonitions. The Kotzker restricted me, debunked cherished attitudes. From the Baal Shem I received the gifts of elasticity in adapting to contradictory conditions.

The Baal Shem dwelled in my life like a lamp, while the Kotzker struck like lightning. To be sure, lightning is more authentic. Yet one can trust a lamp, put confidence in it; one can live in peace with a lamp.

The Baal Shem gave me wings; the Kotzker encircled me with chains. I never had the courage to break the chains and entered into joys with my shortcomings in mind. I owe intoxication to the Baal Shem, to the Kotzker the blessings of humiliation.

The Kotzker's presence recalls the nightmare of mendacity. The presence of the Baal Shem is an assurance that falsehood dissolves into compassion through the power of love. The Baal Shem suspends sadness, the Kotzker enhances it. The Baal Shem helped me to refine my sense of immediate mystery; the Kotzker warned me of the constant peril of forfeiting authenticity. . . .[42]

My origin was in Mezbizh [the town of the Besht]. It gave me nourishment. Following the advice of the old Chortkover Rebbe, Rabbi David Moses, the uncle and second husband of my father's mother, my father settled in Warsaw. There I spent my younger years among Kotzker Hasidim. I am the last of the generation, perhaps the last Jew from Warsaw, whose soul lived in Mezbizh but whose mind was in Kotzk.[43]

Some idea of how Heschel intended to proceed in his work on the Baal Shem comes from an early outline of the book (or part of the book) that he showed me:

1. The Love of God
2. Love for Israel—Love for Evil-Doers
3. Descending into Hell [to Redeem the Sinner]; Self-Sacrifice
4. [Faith?] in the Tzaddik
5. Humility
6. Evil
7. The Value of the Common Deed
8. The Relation to [?]
9. Messiah
10. Sadness
11. Strictness in Observing the Law
12. Truth
13. The Hasid
14. To Study Musar
15. The Besht on Himself
16. The Talmudic Sages
17. Bodily Movement [in Prayer]
18. "Serve Him in All Your Ways"
19. Limits of the Way of the Besht
20. Yearning
21. The Study of Torah
22. The Tzaddik

This outline is, of course, neither complete nor final. The topics, for example, seem not to be arranged in any particular order. No provision is made, moreover, for the historical studies contained in *The Circle of the Baal Shem Tov* that, in revised form, were presumably to form the first part of the work. But what is significant about the outline is that it enables one to contrast Heschel's view of what should constitute the main subjects of Hasidism with that of other scholars.

Heschel did not, as I have noted, complete the work on the Besht that he had planned. One would have wished to possess a comprehensive statement from him, even a single substantial essay, on the meaning of Hasidism. Unfortunately, almost all of his published Hasidic research is of a technical nature. He rarely even lectured on the subject and only once, at the end of his life, did he offer a formal course

on Hasidism at the Jewish Theological Seminary. His scanty
lecture notes, however, do provide brilliant, if all too brief,
insights. At one point he even hints at the reasons for his
reticence. "Young boys are shy," his notes read, "too shy to
lecture on Hasidism. It is too personal. Too intimate. I remained a boy even after becoming a man!"

Besieged by controversy, Hasidism had emerged in the
eighteenth century as a revival movement that engendered
bitter opposition. Its early writings, such as the *Toldot Ya'akov
Yosef* (Korzec [Koretz], 1780), were largely polemical, at-
tacking not only the decline of Judaism into legalism and
asceticism, but also the corruption of Jewish life itself. To
correct the malaise, Hasidism boldly proposed a new type of
leader, the tzaddik, a new stress on one's service to God
which was not limited to Torah study and worship but embraced "all one's ways," and a new mood of joy and exaltation. Along with this program came the daring establishment
of separate synagogues. A furious clash of forces followed,
producing a polemical literature from the Mitnagdim, as the
opponents of the Hasidim were called.

Though the Hasidim, at first separatists themselves and
later excluded by the ruling group, finally rejoined the general community, the remnants of the early opposition never
disappeared. The bitterness that provoked the excommunications of the first generations in the eighteenth century was
still felt in the twentieth. Its tone could be heard in the anti-
Hasidic satire in the East and the aggressively critical reports
by historians in the West. If Hasidim were drunkards, and
tzaddikim little deities dabbling in witchcraft,[44] then it
should come as no surprise that the Besht himself was the
object of stinging jibes. "Ignoramus" and "sorcerer" were
the two terms most commonly applied to him. In an atmosphere in which Western scholars, such as Heinrich Graetz,
were so critical of Hasidism, it was natural that disturbing
questions would continue to be raised: Did the Baal Shem,
in fact, ever live? Do we possess any evidence about him
from contemporary sources, apart from the hagiography that
accumulated after his death? What do we know of his early

followers? What was their relationship to the Frankists and the Sabbatean heresy?[45]

Adored by some and reviled by others, the subject of miracle legends and scurrilous gossip, the inspiration for subsequent communities of the faithful as well as decrees of excommunication, the Baal Shem himself seemed shrouded in mystery. How to get behind the legend to the man? If an historian of Polish Jewry of the distinction of Mayer Balaban despaired in the 1920s and 1930s of finding any verifiable historical evidence about the founder of Hasidism,[46] consider the difficulties that confronted scholars after the Holocaust had destroyed most of the primary sources as well as the movement's living tradition.

Heschel felt it vital that the historical basis for the rise of Hasidism be established to whatever extent it was still possible. To do so meant examining the entire eighteenth-century rabbinic literature for occasional references to and hints of the early Hasidic figures. The libraries of Hebrew Union College and, especially, of the Jewish Theological Seminary provided him with a unique opportunity for a systematic and thorough review. His work was severely hampered by the disastrous fire at the latter institution in 1966 which destroyed or made unavailable many of the rare volumes he needed. With the help of the book dealer Jaker Biegeleisen, Heschel also began to rebuild his own Hasidic library, though he could not replace the valuable material, including rare manuscripts, he had lost in Europe. In 1949, aware of the presence in America of some of the central figures of the Hasidic remnant who had survived, he founded the YIVO Hasidic Archives, which functioned under his guidance and was directed by Moses Shulvass, his friend from Warsaw and Berlin, to search out what could still be salvaged. Heschel believed that there was a reliable oral tradition going back to the earliest Hasidic period, if only one knew where to look and how to listen. The YIVO Archives were, therefore, used as well for fieldwork and oral histories.[47]

In Heschel's relentless search, no document that might illuminate the origins of Hasidism was overlooked. Even rare and early Polish periodicals were scrutinized. Scholars who brought him their discoveries in this field almost always found that Heschel had been there before them. By exhaustively exploring the literature of the early eighteenth century for new information and by re-examining known material and allusive oral traditions, Heschel sought to move toward the establishment of an historical understanding of the Besht and the foundations of the Hasidic movement. The major results of his early work are the four essays collected in *The Circle of the Baal Shem Tov*, which I edited and partially translated.[48] These studies, originally published in Hebrew and Yiddish, represent the first serious attempt to chart the lives and describe the teachings of the exceptional personalities who made up the intimate circle the Besht had gathered about him as disciples, colleagues, or both. These monographs constitute an indispensable corpus of research preliminary to a proper understanding of the Besht, the founder of Hasidism. If the intended work was planned in two volumes—the first to deal with the history and the second the teachings of the Besht—these four essays would have supplied much of the material for the first volume.

They are:

"Rabbi Pinhas of Korzec [Koretz]" (Hebrew) (*Alei 'Ayin: The Salman Schocken Jubilee Volume* [Jerusalem: Schocken, 1948–1952], pp. 213–44);

"Reb Pinkhes Koritzer" (Yiddish) (*YIVO Bleter*, 33 [1949], 9–48);

"Rabbi Gershon Kutover: His Life and Immigration to the Land of Israel" (Hebrew) (*Hebrew Union College Annual*, 23, No. 2 [1950–51], 17–71);

"Rabbi Nahman of Kosów, Companion of the Baal Shem" (Hebrew) (*The Harry A. Wolfson Jubilee Volume*, ed. Saul Lieberman et al. [New York: American Academy for Jewish Research, 1965], pp. 113–41); and

"Rabbi Isaac of Drobitch" (Hebrew) (*Hado'ar Jubilee Volume* [New York: Hado'ar, 1957], pp. 86–94).

Four (or five, if we include Rabbi Moses of Kuty) of the leading figures in the group associated early with the Besht

are discussed in these essays. A number of almost equal importance are not. Heschel did not give us portraits of others
from the Besht's circle, such as Rabbi Nahman of Horodenka
(grandfather of Rabbi Nahman of Bratslav), whose early ascent to Palestine helped set a pattern among Hasidism for
the love of the Land;[49] or Rabbi Jacob Joseph of Polonnoye,
the chief literary disciple of the Besht, whose books are the
main record of the Baal Shem's teachings;[50] or of Rabbi Dov
Ber, the Maggid of Miedzyzrecz (Mezeritch) who succeeded
to the leadership of the movement after the death of the
Besht; or of Rabbi Judah Leib Pistener.[51] No doubt, Heschel
intended eventually to deal with these and other figures. I
have located some significant unpublished material in his
files dealing with these and other personalities which have
yet to be examined.

Strictly speaking, none of the figures Heschel has described in these essays can simply be called a "disciple" of
the Besht's. Rabbi Nahman and Rabbi Pinhas, critics at first,
became disciples who were also colleagues, while Rabbi
Isaac of Drohobycz seems to have remained somewhat distant until the end. (His son Rabbi Yehiel Mikhel of Zloczew,
on the other hand, became one of the most fervent fighters
for the way of the Besht. It was before his house in Brod
that the first Hasidic book, *Toldot Ya'akov Yosef*, by Rabbi
Jacob Joseph of Polonnoye, was publicly burned.) In any
case, those who composed the circle of the Besht did not
submerge their individuality to the Besht: at times they were
partners, at times opponents, at times followers. What each
of them shared in common was the possession of immense
personal talents and their role as the conscious object of the
Besht's missionary efforts.

Prior to Heschel's studies, these figures had been vague
and unclear. Some, like Rabbi Gershon of Kuty, Rabbi Nahman of Kosów, and Rabbi Isaac of Drohobycz (Drobitch),
were occasionally quoted or told about; only Rabbi Pinhas
of Korzec [Koretz] had left a small body of teachings. In
Heschel's adept hands, these men are revealed as formidable
scholars and striking personalities who, no doubt, would

have played a role in any period of Jewish history. In reading these essays, one beholds the image of historical figures and not simply legendary ghosts.

Heschel's thorough examination of eighteenth-century rabbinic literature enabled him to add important facts to what was already known. The close relationship between the earliest members of the "circle" of the Besht and such significant personalities of the time as Rabbi Hayim Hakohen Rapoport of Lwów, Rabbi Meir Margoliot of Lwów and Ostro, Rabbi Eleazer Rokeah of Amsterdam, and Rabbi Ezekiel Landau of Prague is confirmed and explored in Heschel's studies. That the brother-in-law of the Baal Shem, Rabbi Gershon of Kuty, emerges as one of the central figures of his time, suggests a re-evaluation of our understanding of his role in eighteenth-century Jewish history as well as of the role of certain other Hasidic figures. Similarly, that Rabbi Gershon was a halakhic authority respected by the important Rabbi Ezekiel Landau of Prague and by Rabbi Jonathan Eybeschütz points to his role as a communal figure who was later accepted as a leading representative of Palestinian Jewry. Heschel presents a fascinating picture of Rabbi Gershon in the then notable Constantinople Jewish community where Ashkenazim and Sephardim esteemed and worked with one another. The position of Rabbi Gershon can be better appreciated through our new knowledge that a person of such eminence as the wealthy printer and regular visitor to the sultan's court, Moses Soncino, who "administered the funds raised by R. Ezekiel Landau in Poland for the Ashkenazim in Jerusalem," was a close friend of Rabbi Gershon's and, in fact, acted as intermediary in the correspondence between the Besht and Rabbi Gershon. Rabbi Gershon traveled to the Land of Israel from Constantinople accompanied by Rabbis Abraham and Isaac Rosanes, among the most noted leaders of the community. Soon after his arrival, Rabbi Gershon was offered the post of rabbi of the Ashkenazic community of Jerusalem. Heschel's long article, marked by new insights and suggestions, has encouraged considerable further research into Rabbi Gershon Kutover's role in eighteenth-

century Palestine. Persuasive evidence is now available that
the early Hasidic leaders occupied a more important position
than was formerly believed among the pilgrims of the period.

It is in the essay on Rabbi Gershon that Heschel published
an important discovery: a reference to the Besht made during his lifetime by Rabbi Meir Teomim, the head of the
Yeshivah in Lubartów (Levertof) and father of the noted
Talmudist and author of *Peri Megadim*, who writes: "I have
seen a letter from the Holy Land, written by the Hasid, our
master, R. Gershon, may his light continue to shine, wrote
to his renowned [*mefursam*] brother-in-law, Baal Shem Tov,
may his light continue to shine. . . ." The source of this
statement, a Talmudist and father of a halakhic authority, the
term used, *hamefursam*, and the fact that it is one of the very
few contemporary references to the Besht, "refutes the
claims by certain scholars that the founder of Hasidism lived
in some remote corner of the Jewish world and was unknown during his lifetime to all but a very small circle."[52]

Apart from Heschel's contribution to the history of Hasidism in these essays is his analysis of Hasidic thought. His essay
on Rabbi Pinhas of Korzec (Koretz), for example, delineates
the ideological conflict that occurred early in the history of
the movement, in which each side claimed that it possessed
the true meaning of the Besht's legacy. The Maggid of
Miedzyrzecz (Mezeritch) had stressed the centrality of Kabbalah and established *devekut* (cleaving to God) as the highest
goal. For him, the awareness that all is God would lead man
to understand that this world is but so many veils that must
be cast aside to enter into the divine embrace. His language
is strongly Lurianic, with spiritual ascent beyond time and
place the all-consuming goal. For Rabbi Pinhas, on the
other hand, the stress is elsewhere. This world is no illusion.
It is the place, and now is the time, that man must labor
diligently and unremittingly to perfect himself. To escape the
world is to violate the Psalmist's admonition that one must
first "turn from evil" and only then "do good." Rabbi Pinhas, who had favored Rabbi Jacob Joseph of Polonnoye and

not the Maggid as successor to the Besht, emphasized moral virtue and simple faith.

These essays are not all of a single type. The articles on Rabbi Gershon of Kuty, Rabbi Pinhas of Korzec, and Rabbi Nahman of Kosów are finished works. The essay on Rabbi Isaac of Drohobycz, which did not appear in a scholarly journal, is less structured. Published in Hebrew and Yiddish and in various stages of completeness, the essays that constitute *The Circle* should be understood as preliminary studies that would undoubtedly have been edited or recast to make up part of the work on the Besht that Heschel had planned.

Descendant of a Hasidic dynasty and heir of the living tradition at its most vital source, master of the philosophical and historical-critical method of the West, and possessing unusual creative gifts, Heschel was perhaps the one scholar who might have given us the definitive work on Hasidism.

NOTES

1. This paragraph is drawn from Heschel's lectures.

2. A composite from "Hasidism," 14–16; and *A Passion for Truth*, pp. 3–7.

3. One of the few who have commented on Hasidism's creativity came from an unexpected source, a leading *maskil*, the rationalist, Zionist, and Hebraist Ahad Haam (Asher Ginzberg), d. 1927. "We must admit," he wrote, "that if we want to find original Hebrew literature today, we must turn to the literature of Hasidism; there rather than in the literature of *Haskalah* one occasionally encounters (in addition to much that is purely fanciful) true profundity of thought which bears the mark of original Jewish genius" (*Al Parashat Derakhim* [Berlin: Dvir, 1913], vol. 2, p. 29).

4. More explicit cases of the way Hasidic sources are used in Heschel's writings are abundant. For example, the standing title Heschel chose for his youthful volume of Yiddish poems, *Der Shem Hameforash: Mentsh* (Man: The Ineffable Name of God), can be traced to Hasidic-kabbalistic origins. According to a form of gematria (which uses the numerical equivalents of letters to provide

meanings) introduced by the kabbalists that permitted "filling," *milui 'alafim*, where each letter of a Hebrew word receives the numerical value not of the letter itself but of the name of the letter "filled with alefs," the value of the ineffable Name, YHVH (*Yod He Va'v He'*) becomes 45 (= 20 + 6 + 13 + 6), which is equivalent to the simple gematria of the Hebrew *adam* or "man" (= 1 + 4 + 40 = 45)! Thus, through the process of gematria, "man is the ineffable Name of God" (*Keter Shem Tov* [Brooklyn: Kehot, 1972], p. 74, §292).

A further study in Hasidism is Heschel's "Unknown Documents in the History of Hasidism" (Yiddish), *YIVO Bleter*, 36 (1952), 113–35.

5. See Heschel, "Unknown Documents."

6. Ibid.

7. Gershom Scholem; see his *Sabbatai Sevi: The Mystical Messiah, 1626–1676* (Princeton, N.J.: Princeton University Press, 1973).

8. See Salo Baron, "Steinschneider's Contribution to Historiography," *Alexander Marx Jubilee Volume* (New York: Jewish Theological Seminary, 1950), English section, p. 95.

9. Elkan Adler, *Jews in Many Lands* (Philadelphia: Jewish Publication Society, 1905), pp. 50–55.

10. Ibid., pp. 12–13.

11. Abraham Joshua Heschel, *Kotzk: In Gerangel far Emesdikeit* (Kotzk: The Struggle for Integrity), 2 vols. (Tel Aviv: Hamenora, 1973), pp. 7–10.

12. "Hasidism," 14–16.

13. A reference to this problem is found in the introduction to *Teshu'ot Hen* by Gedalia of Linitz, one of the earliest followers of the Besht. The editor of the book, a disciple of Rabbi Gedalia's and a son of the author of *Shivhey Habesht* (In Praise of the Baal Shem Tov, 1815, the first hagiography of the Besht), explains that difficulties in comprehending the text may be due to the profundity of the ideas, the errors of the printer, and the limits of his own understanding in transcribing the text. "Or perhaps the meaning of the author was altered in [my] translating from one language [Yiddish] to another [Hebrew], and it was as a 'tongue of stammerers' to me. For it is known that the task of translating from one tongue to another is considerable, in that care must be taken neither to add nor to detract from the intent of the author" (*Teshu'ot Hen* [Berditchev, 1816; repr. Jerusalem: S. Reifen, 1964], p. 15]).

14. A century ago Solomon Schechter believed that Hasidic literature consisted of some "200 volumes." See his *The Chassidim* (London: Jewish Chronicle, 1887), p. 22. The Mosad Harav Kook of Jerusalem, under the general editorship of Dr. Yitzhak Raphael and the authorship of Shalom H. Parush, began to publish a bibliography of Hasidic literature, only the first volume of which, unfortunately, appeared in 1980). See also the fine translation and commentary of Rabbi Nahum of Chernobyl's *Light of the Eyes* by Arthur Green, published by Paulist Press in 1982.

15. Abraham Joshua Heschel, "The Two Great Traditions: The Sephardim and the Ashkenazim," *Commentary*, 5 (1948), 420–21.

16. Ismar Elbogen, *Der jüdische Gottesdienst in seiner geschichtlichen Entwicklung* (Leipzig: Fock, 1913), p. 392; *Jewish Liturgy: A Comprehensive History*, trans. Raymond P. Scheindlin (Philadelphia: Jewish Publication Society, 1993), p. 295.

17. A. Freimann, *Katalog der Judaica* (Frankfurt: Lehrberger, 1922), p. ix. Also listed under this rubric are the Sadducees and the Pharisees.

18. Contrary to the standard division of nineteenth-century Judaism into two movements, "Reform and Rabbinism," Schechter, in an early unpublished review, divided it into three: The "Mystic Movement" of Hasidism; the "Wissenschaft Movement," represented by the Gaon of Vilna, Krochmal, Rappoport, and Zunz; and "the Rational Movement," associated with Reform (R. Fine, "Solomon Schechter and the Ambivalence of Jewish Wissenschaft" [*Judaism* (Winter 1997), 18–19]).

19. E.g., M. Wilensky, "Some Notes on Rabbi Israel Loebel's Polemic Against Hasidism," *Proceedings of the American Academy for Jewish Research* (PAAJR), 30 (1962), 141–51; Y. Eliach, "The Russian Dissenting Sects and Their Influence on Israel Baal Shem Tov, Founder of Hasidism," ibid., 36 (1968), 57–81; E. Etkes, "The System of R. Hayim of Volozhin as a Response of the Community of the Mitnagdim to Hasidism" (Hebrew), ibid., 39 (1972), 1–46 (Hebrew Section); J. Weiss, "The Great Maggid's Theory of Contemplative Magic," *Hebrew Union College Annual*, 31 (1960), 137–48.

20. Dov Ber, Maggid of Miedzyrzecz (Mezeritch), *Maggid Devarav Leya'akov*, ed. and commentary by Rivkah Schatz-Uffenheimer (Jerusalem: Hebrew University Press, 1976).

21. *The Earth Is the Lord's*, p. 10.

22. David Biale, *Gershom Scholem* (Cambridge, Mass.: Harvard

University Press, 1979), p. 46. See Martin Buber, "Jüdische Wissenschaft," *Die Welt*, 11–12 (October 1901); *Jüdische Bewegung* (Berlin: Jüdische Verlag, 1920), vol. 1, pp. 48–58.

23. Biale, *Gershom Scholem*, p. 11; translation has been emended.

24. See both Gershom Scholem's "M. Buber's Interpretation of Hasidism," in *The Messianic Idea in Judaism* (New York: Schocken Books, 1971), pp. 227–51; and his "Martin Buber's Conception of Judaism," in *On Jews and Judaism in Crisis* (New York: Schocken Books, 1976), pp. 126–72; Rivkah Schatz-Uffenheimer, "Man's Relation to God and the World in Buber's Rendering of the Hasidic Teaching," in *The Philosophy of Martin Buber*, ed. Paul Schilpp and Maurice Friedman (La Salle, Ill.: Open Court, 1967), pp. 403–35; Martin Buber, "Replies to My Critics: On Hasidism," in *Philosophy of Martin Buber*, pp. 731–41; Biale, *Gershom Scholem*, pp. 165–69; Martin Buber, "Interpreting Hasidism," *Commentary*, 36, No. 3 (1963), 218–25; Maurice Friedman, *Martin Buber's Life and Work*, 3 vols.(New York: E. P. Dutton: 1981–1983), index.

25. Biale, *Gershom Scholem*, p. 48. Cf. Stanley Nash, "The Psychology of Dynamic Self-Negation in a Modern Writer, Shai Hurwitz (1861–1922)," PAAJR, 44 (1977), 81–93. See also Stanley Nash, *In Search of Hebraism: Shai Hurwitz and His Polemics in the Hebrew Press* (Leiden: Brill, 1980).

26. For an example of the attractiveness of Sabbateanism to a contemporary novelist, see Isaac Bashevis Singer, *A Young Man in Search of Love* (Garden City, N.Y.: Doubleday, 1978), p. 7. Cf. Samuel H. Dresner, "Is Bashevis Singer a Jewish Writer?" *Midstream*, 27, No. 3 (1980), 42–47.

27. Cf. Biale, *Gershom Scholem*, pp. 155, 172–74, 192–93, and the bibliography cited there. For Buber's response to Scholem's strictures, see Buber, "Replies to My Critics," pp. 731–41, and above, note 23.

28. M. Piekarz, *Bimey Tzemihat Hahasidut* (Jerusalem: Mosad Bialik, 1978). A more polemical approach is adopted by H. Lieberman, "How Jewish 'Researchers' Explore Hasidism" (Hebrew), *Ohel Rahel* (Brooklyn: Empire Press, 1980), vol. 1, pp. 1–49. Cf. Gershom Scholem, *Devarim Bago* (Tel Aviv: Am Oved, 1975), p. 300, n. 20.

See also Eliezer Schweid, "Mysticism and Judaism According to Gershom Scholem" (Hebrew), *Jerusalem Studies in Jewish Thought*, Supplement 2 (1983); R. Shatz, "Gershom Scholem's Interpretation of Hasidism as an Expression of His Philosophy of Idealism"

(Hebrew), in *Gershom Scholem: The Man and His Work* (Hebrew) (Jerusalem: Israel National Academy for Science/Magnes Press–Mosad Bialik), pp. 48–63.

29. "Buber is dissatisfied with Hasidism because it does not expand the realm of revelation," argues Rivkah Schatz-Uffenheimer, "and in this he sees its failure. . . . [But], if Hasidism had been more universal and had dared to broaden the 'horizon of revelation,' instead of confining itself from the start to the revelation in the Torah, it would have achieved this greatness at the price of antinomianism . . . and is it not thus that we must understand Buber's position?" ("Man's Relation to God and the World," p. 419). In a letter to Franz Rosenzweig, Martin Buber wrote that he discontinued religious observances after he became bar mitzvah, at the age of thirteen, and Gershom Scholem testified that "the early Buber developed a deep aversion to the Law, to *halakha* in all its forms." Buber was a "man who with complete radicalism stood aloof from the institutions of Judaism as a cult, and whom nobody ever saw in a synagogue during the almost thirty years he lived in Israel" (Martin Buber, *Briefwechsel aus sieben Jahrzehnten*, ed. Grete Schaeder [Heidelberg: L. Schneider, 1972], vol. 3, p. 141; Gershom Scholem, "Martin Buber's Conception of Judaism," in *On Jews and Judaism in Crisis* [New York: Schocken Books, 1976], p. 129; see also pp. 133–34. Cf. Franz Rosenzweig, "The Builders: Concerning the Law," in *On Jewish Learning*, ed. Nahum N. Glatzer [New York: Schocken Books, 1955], pp. 72–92; Ernst A. Simon, "Martin Buber and the Faith of Israel" [Hebrew], *Divre 'iyun mukdashim le-Mordekhai Martin Buber* [Contemplations dedicated to Mordechai Martin Buber on the occasion of his eightieth birthday] [Jerusalem: Magnes, 1958], pp. 13–56; Arthur Cohen, "Martin Buber and Judaism," in *Leo Baeck Yearbook 25* [London: Secker & Warburg, 1980], pp. 287–300; Nahum N. Glatzer, "Reflection on Buber's Impact on German Jewry," in *Leo Baeck Yearbook 25*, pp. 301–309).

30. Biale, *Gershom Scholem*, pp. 80, 98. Other distinguished scholars of Hasidism are Moshe Idel, Rachel Elior, Zev Gris, Gedalia Nigal, Louis Jacobs, Isaiah Tishbi, and Meir Orion.

31. Preface to Dresner, *The Zaddik*, pp. 7–8.

32. *Kotzk*, pp. 7–10.

33. Abraham Joshua Heschel, *Between God and Man: From the Writings of Abraham J. Heschel*, ed. Fritz A. Rothschild (New York: Harper & Brothers, 1959; rev. repr. New York: Free Press, 1965).

34. An examination of the topics selected for doctoral dissertations in Jewish studies during the past thirty years unfortunately
confirms Heschel's concern.

35. Quotations for which no sources are given come from my
conversations with Heschel or from family members.

36. That is, Rabbi Israel. He was the son of Rabbi David Moses,
the first Tchortkover rebbe and grandson of the famed Rabbi Israel
of Ruzhin, after whom he was named. David Moses of Tchortkov
was married later in life to his niece, Leah-Rachel, the daughter of
his brother, Shalom Joseph, and Heschel's father's mother, both
she and David Moses having been widowed from their first
spouses. Thus, Heschel's grandmother, Leah-Rachel, was both the
daughter-in-law of the Ryzhiner and his granddaughter. Indeed,
David Moses died in her arms in 1903. After the death of her first
husband, Rabbi Abraham Joshua Heschel of Miedzibosh, Heschel's
grandfather, Leah-Rachel brought her son, Heschel's father, to the
court of the Tchortkov, where he was raised. Since Rabbi Israel of
Ruzhin was the great-grandson of the Maggid of Mezritch and
knew intimately those who knew the Maggid, and since Heschel's
father grew up in the house of the Tchortkover, and since the
oral record was handed down from generation to generation with
extraordinary care, this is an instance, which Heschel once cited in
conversation with me, of how reliable traditions going back to the
earliest generations of Hasidism, to the Besht himself, were available to him. It is likewise why, in gathering material for the YIVO
Hasidic Archives, he believed he could find similar authentic material. In fact, it was over this issue—whether searching for such
material should be a priority—that the chief researcher for the Archive, Dr. M. Shulvass, resigned. Cf. A. Twerski, *The Genealogy of
Tchernobl and Ruzhin* (Hebrew) (Lublin, 1938), p. 120.

In addition to being descended on his father's side from Rabbi
Abraham Joshua Heschel of Apt, Rabbi Israel of Ruzhin, and
Rabbi Dov Ber of Mezritch, Heschel counted on his mother's side,
Rabbi Levi Yitzhak of Berditchev, Rabbi Shlomo of Karlin, and
Rabbi Pinhas of Koretz. See the detailed genealogy in Edward K.
Kaplan and Samuel H. Dresner, *Abraham Joshua Heschel* (New
Haven, Conn.: Yale University Press, 1998).

37. Cf. H. Rabinowicz, *The World of Hasidism* (London: Valentine, 1970), pp. 164–66; A. Bromberg, *Hasidic Leaders* (Hebrew)
(Jerusalem: Hamakhon Lehasidut, 1963), vol. 20, pp. 124–68.

38. Heschel's appreciation of his uncle is confirmed by other

sources. So admiring was he of him that the Gerer Rebbe, the ranking Hasidic leader in Poland, used to send his Hasidim to visit the Novominsker and would himself call upon him whenever the Gerer was in Warsaw. Evidence of the friendship between the two is found in a letter, which I have seen, from the Gerer Rebbe to the Novominsker after the death of the Gerer's wife, thanking him for his encouragement to proceed with a second marriage. When the Gerer Rebbe sought someone to head the powerful Agudas Yisroel organization, he remarked that there was only one person in all of Poland whom he could recommend without qualification: the Novominsker Rebbe; and when his followers asked whom they should consult upon his departure for a visit to the Holy Land, the Gerer again responded: the Novominsker. Hillel Zeitlin observed, "Whenever I felt depressed and needed to repent, I visited the rabbi of Novominsk." The chief rabbi of Tel Aviv, Rabbi Yedidiah Frankel, said, "The picture I have in my mind of a perfect tzaddik is the rabbi of Nomominsk. His profound wisdom, his constant learning, the depth of his kabbalistic mastery, his majestic face, the smile which never left his face, his love of all Israel, his refusal to utter a critical word about another, were unforgettable" (Bromberg, *Hasidic Leaders*).

39. Hebrew: *shmone esre*; the long-standing prayer or *amida* is said with a swaying motion of the body. Beillis, "The Beginnings of Yung Vilno," in *Die goldene Keit*, pp. 18–19; cf. E. Schulman, *Yung Vilne, 1929–1939* (Yiddish) (New York: Getseltn, 1946).

40. Heschel's plan is indicated in the introductory note to his first published essay on the history of Hasidism, the Yiddish study "Reb Pinkhes Koretzer" (*YIVO Bleter*, 33 [1949], 9), which he described as "a chapter from the author's work on *the Besht and his circle*" (emphasis added). By July 1947 Heschel had completed his essays on Rabbi Pinhas of Koretz and Rabbi Gerson of Kutov (ibid., 48).

41. For the 1963 interview with him in which the Yiddish journalist Gershon Jacobson, recorded Heschel's recollections as a newcomer to America, see above, pp. 23–24.

42. *A Passion for Truth*, pp. xiii–xv.

43. *Kotzk*, p. 10.

44. Heinrich Graetz, *History of the Jews* (Philadelphia: Jewish Publication Society, 1898), vol. 5, pp. 375–81.

45. On these movements, see Scholem's *Sabbetai Sevi*.

46. "According to Balaban, all that is left to us concerning the

life of the founder of the Hasidic movement is pure legend. To him, therefore, no responsible historian should attempt to write an historical treatise on this topic. 'A legend is a piece of folk poetry and it should not be dissected. We must take the legend as it is, or not use it at all.' There are no historical facts whatsoever against which to test these legends about the Baal Shem Tov. . . . Balaban is dubious as to whether any genuine evidence relating to the founder of the Hasidic movement will ever be found. 'Israel Baal Shem Tov was a simple man. He did not participate in the public life of the Jewish community, and did not come into contact with the leading personalities of his age. He did not compose books himself and did not write introductions to the books of others.' Neither did he engage in business activities nor have any communication with the Polish noblemen. There is therefore nowhere to look for traces of his activities. All we have is a multitude of legends, which often contradict each other" (I. Biderman, *Mayer Balaban: Historian of Polish Judaism* [New York: Biderman Book Committee, 1976], pp. 204–205; cf. M. Balaban, "Hasidut," *Hetekufa*, 18 [1923], 488. Balaban's strict delimitation of the role of legend was made, in part, in reviewing the exaggerated claims of S. Setzer's biography of the Besht in the periodical *Bicher Velt*, 1, Nos. 4–5 [1922], 406–407).

Balaban's general view of Hasidism was one of disapproval. He claimed that Hasidism had a negative influence upon family life and was one of the major causes of the decline of Polish Jewish culture. Summarizing Balaban's view, Biderman writes that "Polish Jewish culture . . . came to fruition during the seventeenth century, later to deteriorate under the twofold impact of the misfortunes which beset Polish Jewry from outside and the decay brought about by the mystical and Hasidic movements from within the community" (p. 174). At least three factors must be considered in assessing Balaban's disapprobation: (*a*) the highly critical views of Heinrich Graetz; (*b*) the testimony of the historian Moses Shulvass, Balaban's student, that Balaban's knowledge of Hebrew did not allow him to master the sources sufficiently to gain a proper understanding of Hasidism; and (*c*) Balaban's descent from a family of Mitnagdim. One ancestor was a co-signer, with the rabbi of Lwów, of the 1792 excommunication of the Hasidim, while Balaban's grandfather "was known for his opposition to the Hasidism and was a principal supporter of Rabbi Ornstein of Lemberg [i.e., Lwów] from 1804 to 1839," a leading opponent of the Hasidic movement. "Opposition to Hasidism was characteristic of the Balaban family tradition."

One of the major objectives of Heschel's studies was to refute the point of view represented by Balaban, arguing, that, indeed, "there are . . . historical facts . . . against which to test these legends about the Baal Shem Tov," to the point of affirming that the Besht did, in fact, "come into contact with leading personalities of his age." Meanwhile, Moshe Rosman has discovered documents from the Polish archives of Medzibosh establishing the Besht's residence there and the importance of this residence (Moshe Rosman, *Founder of Hasidism* [Berkeley: University of California Press, 1966]).

47. See Heschel's introductory remarks of to his "Unknown Documents in the History of Hasidism."

48. Abraham J. Heschel, *The Circle of Baal Shem Tov: Studies in Hasidism*, ed. Samuel H. Dresner (Chicago: The University of Chicago Press, 1985; rev. ed. New York: Jewish Theological Seminary, 1998).

49. See "Unknown Documents in the History of Hasidism," 115–19.

50. See Dresner, *The Zaddik*.

51. He was held in such esteem by Jacob Joseph of Polonnoye that he published his eulogy of him (*Toldot Ya'akov Yosef* [Koretz: Katz, 1780], p. 92d).

52. See *Circle of the Baal Shem Tov*, pp. 71–76, 98–99.

3

Halakha

The Left

SEVEN YEARS AFTER Heschel had left the Hebrew Union College for Reform Judaism to become a member of the faculty of the conservative Jewish Theological Seminary, he was invited to the annual convention of the organization of the Reform rabbinate, the Central Conference of American Rabbis. That invitation would hardly have been made while he was still teaching in Cincinnati, where his traditional lifestyle, such as observing Kashrut and Shabbat, in addition to his "spiritual" interests, no doubt contributed to his receiving only a modicum of recognition; but with the subsequent publication of several important books in English and his growing influence in Jewish and non-Jewish circles, the invitation was issued. In that very year Heschel also challenged the convention of the Conservative rabbinate, many of whom had long been under the spell of the religious humanism of Mordecai Kaplan, with his address on prayer in which he argued theology—"the problem of prayer is the problem of God." Now he chose to confront the Reform leaders with their most controversial position, the issue of halakha.

Heschel began by alluding to his own problems with observance of the Law. Perhaps it was an attempt to gain some measure of approval from an audience, critical in any case, and now put on alert upon learning the challenging subject of his address. But could he put at ease a body of listeners who were suspicious of one whose differing views they had held at a distance in the past and who were now preparing to encounter those views face to face, especially a defense of the Law, which they had long ago rejected? On the other hand, there were no doubt many among the younger rabbis who, having experienced the failure of classical Reform to create a passion for Judaism, were willing to give Heschel a hearing. After all, he had not just emerged from a *shtibl* or a yeshivah.

I have remarked that Heschel had left Warsaw at the age of eighteen to attend the secular Real-Gymnasium in Vilna (where he also joined a group of promising Yiddish poets, later to become the famed Yung Vilno) in preparation for his attendance at the University of Berlin, and at the liberal, not the Orthodox, Jewish seminary there.[1] Subsequently he was saved from the Nazis by the visa provided by the Hebrew Union College, which brought him out of Warsaw, to which he had been repatriated, only weeks before the Germans entered, to their school in Cincinnati, where he remained for five years. From this history one could reasonably assume that he had a good understanding of the motivations of those who were troubled by the Law. "In their . . . fear of desecrating the spirit of the divine command," he subsequently wrote, "the Rabbis established a level of observance which, in modern society, is within the reach of exalted souls but not infrequently beyond the grasp of ordinary man."[2]

More than Jewish misgivings, however, was the formidable challenge he experienced in the cultural wealth and dazzling splendor of that greatest metropolis in Western Europe of the late twenties. He recalls this encounter in one of his few autobiographical remarks, which I cited earlier. He tells us with what thirst he came to the university to drink in the teachings of its famed professors, and how gravely confronted he felt by them. In the evenings he would often walk the impressive streets of Berlin framed by powerful architecture and decorated with beautiful parks. One evening during such a walk, while considering which play or lecture to attend, he noticed the sun had set, and he had forgotten to pray the evening service. Upset, he began to pray. At this point he interrupted his report to ask, "Why did I decide to take religious observance seriously . . . ? Why did I pray, although I was not in the mood to pray?"[3]

Heschel used words with precision. When he asks, "Why did I decide to take religious observance seriously?" he is implying that there was another option that he had considered. Heschel's answer to the question he posed, both in this address and in works that followed, constitutes a formidable statement on the meaning of Jewish observance.

Let us consider his answer.

Omitting the evening prayer, he explains, "was not only the failure to pray to God during a whole evening of my life but *the loss of the whole*, the loss of belonging to the spiritual order of Jewish living. . . . [That] order . . . is meant to be, not a set of rituals, but an order of all of man's existence, shaping all his traits, interests and dispositions; 'not so much the performance of single acts, the taking of a step now and then, as the pursuit of a way, being on the way; not so much the acts of fulfilling as the state of being committed to the task, the belonging to an order in which single deeds, aggregates of religious feeling, sporadic sentiments, moral episodes become a part of a complete pattern.' "[4]

In response to Rudolph Harnack's *The Essence of Christianity*, the noted leader of the German Liberal/Reform movement, Rabbi Leo Baeck, wrote a book which he called *The Essence of Judaism* and which was seen as the premier statement of Liberal Judaism. While it is clear that Heschel accepted the notion of such an "essence," that is, a core of beliefs fundamental to and in summary of the Jewish faith, he was at the same time alert to the danger, lest such an abstract of Judaism be perceived as the whole. It is the danger of aggada alone. Ideas, after all, do not dwell in a void: lacking a living medium, removed from the substance out of which they are distilled and the forms through which they may be expressed, even the most precious "essence" can evaporate and disappear: the center may not hold. To make his point, Heschel, as he would often do, told a story:

"A friend of mine used to go to a small, beautiful park in Berlin. He would sit and think and relax. One day a man appeared with a violin and started to play. My friend loved music and had a good understanding of it, but, for the life of him, he could not figure out what the man was playing. There seemed to be no harmony, no melody, no tune. Of course he was tolerant and did nothing to interfere, but this man came every day, playing, playing, and it made no sense. After some time, his patience exhausted, my friend inquired,

'What is the name of the composer whose works you are playing?'

'They have no composer,' he answered.

'What music is it, then?' my friend persisted.

'It is music *überhaupt*—music in general!' "

The vulgar Americanized version of this anecdote is the one about the confused newly elected rabbi who asks—after being advised by the synagogue president not to speak about the Sabbath because of golf, or about Kashrut because of the cost, or about the Hebrew school because of sports—what he *can* preach about—and is told: "Why, Judaism, of course!"

In moments of weakness, when beset by temptation and confusion, when the will is weak and the mind unsteady, even the right ideas alone prove inadequate. One can be more easily guided by the ever-present option of the Law. One need only to reach out and grasp a familiar, cherished mitzvah and be carried along to a clearer future. You give tzedakah, though you may do it for self-promotion; you say the kiddush prayer at the Sabbath table, though you may prefer to watch TV; you go to the synagogue, though you would rather sleep. The *siyata dishmaya* (heavenly grace) that Judaism makes available to mortal, faltering humans flows from the power of a pattern of living touched by the divine.[5]

Furthermore, no society can long abide anarchy. Indeed, anarchy itself is nothing more than the abandonment of one norm for the eventual assumption of another. Heschel once observed to me that a cardinal error of Martin Buber's was his antinomianism—that is, his rejection of the regimen of the halakha in the belief that nothing must restrain the freedom of human response to a particular situation—and cited the example of an Israeli kibbutz. When the kibbutz was established by members of the Zionist youth group whose mentor was Buber, it found itself no longer just a fellowship of young idealists debating a cause or discussing a book, but a living flesh-and-blood community and, as such, in need of a "way," not just a theory. Having rejected the way of Jewish tradition, it adopted that of Marxism. The orthodox character of its left-wing philosophy, though modified over the years, was still so unyielding that, despite second thoughts on the part of the younger generation, the kibbutz refused a family request for a bar mitzvah not too many years ago and directed them to a nearby "religious" colony.

Karl Barth's Pauline-Lutheran position that, because man's sinfulness prevents him from performing good deeds, law must be abandoned in favor of a religion of grace, was labeled "heresy" by Heschel.[6] Though flawed, man *can* perform the mitzvot. Inwardness, admirable in itself, is not enough and can never provide an adequate avenue for religion. "Religion is not the same as spiritualism; what man does in his concrete physical existence is directly relevant to the divine. . . . The innermost chamber must be guarded at the uttermost outposts."[7] If the Greeks stressed right thinking and the Christians right belief, Israel's emphasis was upon right living. What one must do here and now is the core of religion according to the prophets. "What *creed* is in relation to *faith*, the *halacha* is in relation to *piety*. As faith cannot exist without a creed, piety cannot subsist without a pattern of deeds. . . . Judaism is lived in deeds, not only in thoughts." From this vantage point, Judaism can be described, in Heschel's memorable phrase, as "the theology of the common deed."

Religion is not a matter of the heart alone. It embraces life, all of life. "Jewish tradition," wrote Heschel, "maintains that there is no extra-territoriality in the realm of the spirit. Economics, politics, dietetics are" all included. Moreover, "it is in man's intimate rather than public life, in the way he fulfills his physiological functions that character is formed."[8] He argued that in beginning with the finite, we can reach the infinite, and suggested that, instead of a leap of faith, "A Jew is asked to take *a leap of action* . . . to do more than he understands in order to understand more than he does."[9]

Scripture tells us that the people-Israel responded to the rev-elation at Sinai with the words "We shall do and we shall understand" (na'aseh v'nishma). Should the order not be re-versed, first "understanding" and then "doing?" Heschel would often quote the Besht's resolution of this puzzle: in the "doing" (asiah) is the "understanding" (shmiah) (Ex. 24:7).

Heschel rejected the body/mind dualism that the West in-herited from the Greeks in favor of biblical monism whereby body and mind form a single unit. He believed that by re-placing the dominant Greek/German categories of thought with those of the Bible, solutions could be found to many contemporary philosophical problems. Most of his books are an attempt to do just this.[10] One example of biblical monism is the Hebrew word nefesh, which is commonly translated "spirit" or "soul," but, in fact, means body and soul, the entire "person." "Implicitly, the assumption that 'knowl-edge' is cognitive, that one can know something by reading about it or being otherwise informed about it, is fundamental to much of what we do. Our assumption that knowledge is acquired through thought, which is a distinct and localized phenomenon, is at the heart of our entire educational enter-prise." One learns "rationally," with the mind, but also exis-tentionally from "doing." Heschel, of course, is not impugning the importance of knowledge gathered through the mind, but he denies that this is the only form of cognition, arguing that experience, bodily behavior itself, also affords knowl-edge, a different kind of knowledge, knowledge that the mind can often only touch on and hint at. One will never really know what milk tastes like if one has never tasted milk. All the books on what a mother means cannot convey moth-erhood to one who has never known his mother. In the performance of the mitzvah one learns from doing. Judaism stands for the "theology of the common deed."[11]

However, any regimen can fall into the trap of unthinking, mechanical behavior. One way out of that problem is to perform the mitzvah only in inspired moments, only when we feel like it. But, Heschel reminds us, "in abrogating regu-larity we deplete spontaneity."[12] Moments of inspiration are

10 — see pg 118

rare. The mind is often dull, bare, and vapid. "What may seem to be spontaneous is in truth in response to an occasion. The soul would remain silent if not for the summons and reminder of the law. . . . For this reason the Jewish way of life is to reiterate the ritual," to follow a *routine*. It is not only the goal but the way that is important. Thus, Heschel adds, "the very act of going to the house of worship" with regularity "is a song without words." One can and should do what the Law requires, even when one does not feel like doing it, because "The path of loyalty to the routine of sacred living runs along the borderline of the spirit. . . . Routine holds us in readiness for the moments in which the soul enters into accord with the spirit. While love is hibernating, our loyal deeds speak. It is right that . . . good actions should become a habit. . . . A good person is not he who does the right thing, but he who is in the habit of doing the right thing."[13]

Tradition, as Will Herberg put it, is the funded wisdom of the past. We do not create tradition simply by pulling a switch, convening a committee, or contracting a scholar. Tradition is filtered through the ages and takes on the holiness with which generations more pious than ours have invested it. In the oval office of John Kennedy hung the motto: "Whatever it is not necessary to change, it is necessary not to change." *Continuity* is vital, argued Heschel, for "Without solidarity with our forebears, the solidarity with our brothers will remain feeble." We need not simply repeat what was, but "integrat[ing] the abiding teachings and aspirations of the past into our thinking will enable us to be creative. . . . Our way of life must remain such as would be, to some degree, intelligible to Isaiah and Rabbi Yochanan ben Zakkai, to Maimonides and the Baal Shem."[14]

What of those who created that pattern of deeds, who established that continuity which has withstood the ravages of time, who labored in the Law, mastered it, and applied it, whatever the vicissitudes of the land or the age? "In their eyes," Heschel writes in his moving eulogy for East European Jewry:

the world was not a derelict which the creator had abandoned to chance. Life to them was not an opportunity for indulgence, but a mission entrusted to every individual, an enterprise at least as responsible, for example, as the management of a factory. Every man constantly produces thoughts, words, deeds, committing them either to the powers of holiness or the powers of impurity. He is constantly engaged either in building or in destroying. . . .

Scientists dedicate their lives to the study of the habits of insects or the properties of plants. To them every trifle is significant; they inquire diligently into the most intricate qualities of things. [So] the pious Ashkenazic scholars investigated just as passionately the laws that ought to govern human conduct. . . . Wishing to banish the chaos of human existence and to civilize the life of man according to the Torah, they trembled over every move, every breath. . . . Just as the self-sacrificing devotion of the scientist seems torture to the debauchee, so the poetry of rigorism jars on the ears of the cynic. But, perhaps, the question of what benediction to pronounce upon a certain type of food, the problem of matching the material with the spiritual, is more important than is generally imagined.

Man has not advanced very far from the coast of chaos. A frantic call to disorder shrieks in the world. Where is the power that can offset the effect of that alluring call? The world cannot remain a vacuum. We are all either ministers of the sacred or slaves of evil. The only safeguard against constant danger is constant vigilance, constant guidance.[15]

Heschel devised what he called a *pedagogy of return*, a way of reaching and leading the modern Jew to the way of mitzvot. In Heschel's hands, this teaching became reminiscent both of the love of the people Israel (*'ahavat Yisra'el*), exemplified by such of his Hasidic ancestors as Rabbi Levi Yitzhak of Berditchev, as well as of the doctrine of the "descent of the Tzaddik" (*yeridat ha-tzaddik*), by which the Hasidic leader journeys out and down to the people to befriend them and draw them up from the pit of ignorance and error.[16]

Beware, Heschel counseled the American rabbi: neither condemn your congregants too harshly for their lack of knowledge and observance, nor demand too much too soon. Do not confront them with the option of "all" or "nothing." (Rosenzweig had said the question was not "das alles oder das nichts" but "das etwas.") Before passing judgment, one is obligated to try to understand the dilemma of the modern Jew. After returning from a lecture tour, Heschel once observed to me that, considering the discouraging conditions of the Jewish community—the lifeless synagogue, the bar-mitzvah–oriented school, the home drained of Yiddishkeit—it was remarkable that so many American Jews, especially young people, were still open to Jewish ideas. Had he been raised in such an atmosphere, Heschel mused, he wondered if he would have remained an observant Jew! He admired the young Jew who had been given so little of Jewishness and still holds on, as if hoping for something to happen. For all these reasons, Heschel argued, the Jewish leader must establish what he called a *ladder of observance* in which the modern Jew is sought out and met on whatever level his circumstances place him and then be shown how to rise one rung at a time as far as he can go, and even, Heschel would add, a bit further.

Turning from the expository, Heschel sounded a more personal note when not long after his address at the convention of Reform rabbis, the students of The Hebrew Union College, not to be outdone by the rabbis, invited their erstwhile teacher to address them. Now, no longer a member of the faculty of that institution, he felt freer to express himself, even to the point of exhortation.[17] "I am not an halakhist," Heschel told them.

> My field is Aggada. . . . But, remember, there is no aggadah without halakha. There can be no Jewish holiness without Jewish law, at least the essence of Jewish Law.[18] Jewish theology and tefillin go together. . . . Why are you afraid of wearing talis and tefillin every morning, my friends? There was a time when our adjustment to Western civilization was our supreme problem. . . . By now we are well adjusted. . . . Our task today is to adjust Western civilization to Judaism. America, for example, needs Shabbos. What is wrong with

Shabbos, with saying a *brokho* [blessing] every time we eat, with regularity of prayer? What is wrong with spiritual discipline? It is only out of such spiritual discipline that a new manifestation of human existence will emerge. I say *human* and not Jewish existence, because Judaism, which can be very concrete, answers universal problems. It is not a parochial matter to me. I am beset by the same problems that confront a Mohammedan, Christian, or Buddhist. Judaism is an answer to the problems of human living. But it is an answer in a special way. Let us not forfeit the way.

In the question-and-answer period that followed, Heschel became animated:

What is wrong with Jewish Law? . . . What it is wrong with going to a restaurant and being unable to forget that one is a part of the covenant between God and Israel? It may be uncomfortable. It *is* uncomfortable. But what is our motivation if we do not accept halakha? If I am really interested in being reminded of the presence of God, of being reminded that I am part of the eternal people, that I am a Yehudi, that I am almost the ineffable name of God,[19] then I am honored by [the halakha], and I need it. I could not be without it. And I see nothing in the tradition of Reform Judaism to abolish it. European Reform did observe much of the halakha. [The abolition of halakha] was an episode in American Reform Judaism. To reform Jewish Law is one thing, but to do away with it is quite another.

"When I was at the Hebrew Union College," he remarked, finally, turning the onus upon the students,

the issue of halakha was widely discussed. Many sermons were delivered by students calling upon the Central Conference of American Rabbis [the Reform rabbinical body] to revitalize halakha. But I shall tell you a secret. I know many members of the Central Conference. They wait for the student body. It is the student body that could have the courage and vision of bringing about the revitalization of the Jewish spirit. Why do you not do something about it?

Heschel struck another note in this hitherto-unknown address to the Hebrew Union College students, a note that is hardly duplicated in his writings or conversations, because it is a sarcastic critique of the Reform rabbinate. Harsh criticism of others was not in Heschel's vocabulary. For example, he did not respond by name to those who attacked him, believing that his energies should be put to more constructive use. However, after his memorable address on halakha to the Reform rabbis and this invitation by the students of Hebrew Union College, he no doubt wanted to unburden himself of feelings that had been pent up while he was in Cincinnati. Gratitude for having brought him out of Warsaw a few weeks before the Nazi invasion was a primary reason for his former restraint, but also, as mentioned above, he hoped to influence the students in the direction of a more traditional Judaism, such as that of the German Liberal model with which he was familiar from his years in Berlin. American Reform's rejection of halakha, he reminded them, may have only been one stage, an "episode," in its history.

Heschel's frankest statement on the Reform rabbinate and, by implication, with the institution training them, is contained in an anecdote he recounted during that visit to Cincinnati. Essential to returning American Jews to Judaism, and a compelling concern of Heschel's, were knowledgeable and committed rabbis. He understood the fruitful lesson of the Baal Shem Tov that the revival of the depressed Jewry of the eighteenth century depended upon the leader, and, consequently, strove to create a new kind of rabbi, the zaddik. Heschel knew from his upbringing what a true leader was. In his youth, he had been surrounded by exceptional rabbinic figures, was the descendent of many such generations, and was raised to become one himself. Indeed, during his youth it was widely held that he would become *the* leader to save Polish Hasidism.

What of the twentieth-century American rabbi? With the fall of European Jewry and the virtual obliteration of Polish Jewry—for Heschel the heart and mind of European Judaism—he saw as one of his major tasks the training of spiritual leaders who would awaken American Jews to their faith. Heschel had spent five years in Cincinnati where he had

ample time to understand the dilemma of the Reform rabbinate: their "mile-wide, inch-deep" failed education, their
futile attempt to revive worship by ever revising the liturgy,
their misguided notion that spiritual problems can be dealt
with through administrative techniques, and their lack of
passion. After all, how could one succeed with a limited
knowledge of Hebrew, little Talmud or Midrash, a scientific
but not theological training in Bible, and without a commitment to Jewish "learning," to the authority of tradition, and
to the ancestral pattern of Jewish living, but, all the while
assured of being quite prepared to teach and guide one's
congregants? An example of the stifling spiritual atmosphere
that prevailed at the Hebrew Union College is the fact that
during the years I studied there, from 1942 to 1945, I can
hardly remember a student discussion of the Holocaust. Nor
was the topic taken up by any of the public celebrities passing through the city who were invited by the students to
address them.

   With this situation in mind, one can better appreciate the
tale Heschel recounted toward the end of his remarks to the
students during his visit, told with tongue in cheek. "I
would like to tell you a Hasidic story," Heschel began.

   Mishna Peah 8:9 says that "If a beggar evokes pity, pretending
   that he is lame or blind, then he will be punished by really
   becoming lame or blind." Now, there was a great rabbi who
   died well over one hundred years ago by the name of Rabbi
   Simha Bunim of Psyshkha. In those days there were those
   who took the title and played the role of a Hasidic rabbi, but,
   if you will forgive the expression, were really fakers. Painfully
   aware of the situation, Bunim asked, "So, what should be the
   punishment of one who is not worthy of being a rabbi but
   claims to be a rabbi? According to the Mishna, he will become a *real* rabbi! But is that a punishment?"

In answer to that question, Heschel continued, Bunim told
this tale:

   There was a Russian peasant named Mushka. The other peas-
   ants decided to play a joke on him. First they got him good

and drunk, then they dressed him up in the gown of a priest, took him to church, and sat him down on the priest's chair near the altar. Mushka slept peacefully for quite a while. When he awoke, he was still groggy from drink and barely able to move. Though he looked like a priest and was sitting on the priest's chair in church near the altar, he had a growing recollection of just being a peasant! He must be asleep, he thought, only dreaming of being a priest. That thought put him at ease.

But was he really asleep? He noticed that he was able to do certain things, like touching and holding and walking, which sleeping people are unable to do. It must be the other way around, he thought. He is not a sleeping peasant but an awake priest. Anybody can see that. And as to having been a peasant, that must just be a dream he once had.

But this, too, did not make sense. The memory of being a peasant was too real. After all, he felt like a peasant and had only peasant memories.

Now he was thoroughly confused: Was he still asleep, a peasant dreaming that he was a priest, or was he awake, a priest who had only dreamt he was a peasant? In short, was he priest or peasant?

Being very shrewd, Mushka recalled that when he used to go the church, the priest would take out a big book and read it as part of the service. Now, he knew that only the priest was able to read. There was the book before him. He would open it. If he could read the book, it would prove that he was a priest; if not, he would just be a peasant.

He opened the book—and could not read a single word. Alas, that meant that he was a peasant, asleep, just dreaming he was a priest.

But how could that be? After all, his clothes were the clothes of a priest, he was in the church of the priest, sitting on the throne of the priest, and, what is more, he felt fully awake!

Then the answer dawned upon him.

"I am really a priest. And as to my not being able to read—*Who says priests can read?*"

An illiterate priest whose duties require him to be able to read is an embarrassment. So with the rabbi who lacks the knowledge to teach Judaism yet is expected to do so. Don't fool others, said the Rabbi of Kotzk, but, even more, don't fool yourself!

In summary, these are some of the essentials of Heschel's defense of halakha: the insufficiency of inwardness alone; the principle of law is more important than any particular law (halakhiyut vs. a halakha); the theology of the common deed; the leap of action; continuity with our forefathers; loyalty to a routine; living within a spiritual order; no extraterritoriality in the realm of the spirit; constant danger requires constant vigilance; a Jewish answer to universal problems; the ladder of observance; the pedagogy of return; the qualified teacher.

The Right

In the world of post-emancipation Jewry, the rejection of halakha became a rallying cry for classical Reform in the West and for the Jewish movements of secularism and enlightenment in the East. They viewed halakha as repressive, a barrier to their admission into Western culture, a barnacle of a fossilized past. The issue, of course, is still with us, but the tone is no longer shrill, the approach no longer uncompromising. Time, the collapse of the utopias of science and socialism, and especially the Holocaust, which obliterated the centers of traditional Judaism, have encouraged a reconsideration by all parties. Religious anti-traditionalists, along with anti-religious secularists, have muted their objections in part. A new respect for Jewish tradition is manifest.

However, if the left has moderated, the right has revived, expanded, and hardened. Extremism has shifted from one side to the other. Halakhic fundamentalism, expected by many to fade away in the glare of the twentieth century, has resurfaced not only in Israel, which is, after all, the Jewish homeland and the primary refuge for those who survived the Holocaust, but in the least accommodating environment imaginable: enlightened, liberal America. It has done so with a surprising energy that is both admirable and frightening,

continuing to accelerate, intimidating moderates, and claiming to delegitimize centrists.

A few bizarre examples of Jewish legal questions asked in
recent responsa literature gives us a sense of the shocking
extent to which matters have deteriorated: May one partake
in the grace after meals at a United Jewish Appeal dinner if
it is led by a non-Orthodox rabbi? Are Conservative rabbis
heretics? In the event that an Orthodox synagogue is not
available on Rosh Hashana, the New Year, may one go to a
Conservative synagogue just to fulfill the mitzvah of hearing
the blowing of the shofar? May an Orthodox synagogue em-
ploy a scribe to write a Torah or a marriage contract (ketuvah)
or a document of divorce (get) if he has written a Torah for
a Conservative congregation? May one hire a hazan who has
prayed in a Conservative synagogue? Is religious tolerance
grounded in Torah or merely the aping of gentile ways
(hukat hagoyim) and contrary to Jewish teaching?[20] The fact
that such cases are taken sufficiently seriously to be published
is evidence of the menacing spirit abroad in the land.

As the Holocaust plays a role in moving the left to a
greater openness toward tradition, so it contributes to the
rise and the hardening of the extreme right. An example of
this has been the shift from venerating Western culture as
the source of all blessing to vilifying that culture as the source
of Auschwitz. Thus, the teacher in a baal teshuvah yeshivah
sneeringly responded to being told by a new student that he
had majored in Shakespeare at Yale: "Shakespeare! A shikker
goy!" Nor is this the first time in history that Jews have re-
treated into the tightly drawn corners of the ghetto behind
the high walls of the Law. Even in the Talmud, a sage ob-
serves that if you allow yourself to be distracted from the
study of Torah to admire a beautiful tree, you are deserving
of punishment.[21]

Only consider that as far back as the early nineteenth century, Rabbi Jacob (Yokev) Ettlinger, venerated as "the last
Gaon of Germany," could attend a university, as, prior to
the Holocaust, could the late Lubavitcher Rebbe, while
America's best-known talmudist, Rabbi J. B. Soloveitchik,

could receive a doctorate on the philosophy of Hermann Cohen from the University of Berlin in the 1930s, or that faculty members of the Liberal Jewish seminary in Berlin could contribute articles to the *Festschrift* for the chief judge of the Jewish court in Berlin and professor of codes at the Orthodox seminary. The Talmud records that once " 'Aher' [the noted heretic Elisha ben Abuya] was riding upon his horse [in violation of the laws of] the Sabbath with Rabbi Meir walking behind him to learn Torah!"[22] Would such fraternity or such achievements in secular education be possible today after the Holocaust? Even at the "moderate" Yeshiva University, one must search long and hard to find mention of such classic works of scholarship as the monumental fourteen-volume edition of and commentary to the Tosephta by Rabbi Saul Lieberman or the seminal works of Abraham Heschel, because they were associated with a Conservative and not an Orthodox seminary. It is difficult today to conceive of an Israeli rabbi who is university trained or one emerging from a Brooklyn yeshivah with a doctorate in the humanities.[23]

The president of Yeshiva University, Norman Lamm, titled his book *Torah and Culture (Torah Umada)*, in an attempt to assert continuity with the more worldly Orthodox seminaries of Berlin and London. It was not to be. Instead of establishing itself as "middle-of-the-road" Orthodoxy, Yeshiva University has become peripheral to the powerful Brooklyn yeshivot where university studies are taboo. The Westernization of Orthodoxy, best symbolized by the general agreement that Christians are not to be treated as idolaters, with all that implies halakhically, is being questioned today.[24] Indeed, since the Holocaust, Orthodoxy has been steadily moving to a repudiation of its adjustment to Western culture.

For some years now Orthodox rabbis and laymen (including the so-called moderates) refuse to sit with non-Orthodox for almost any purpose. The Synagogue Council of America, the erstwhile all-embracing synagogue body that dealt only with *non*-religious issues, had to disband a few years ago because of the withdrawal of the Orthodox from even such an association. A striking case of the move rightward is found in a study of the eulogies that appeared in right-wing Orthodox publications marking the death of perhaps the single most influential figure in American Orthodoxy, Rabbi J. B. Soloveitchik, who single-handedly trained a generation of rabbis who made Orthodoxy intellectually acceptable to American Jewry. They extended only half-hearted praise, denying Soloveitchik the customary honorific *zekher tzaddik livrakha* ("the memory of the righteous shall be for a blessing"). He is rarely mentioned in these circles today.[25]

Heschel was one of the most persuasive defenders of Jewish tradition, who decried Judaism without halakha as a soul without a body. Yet he was careful to add with equal vigor, that Judaism without aggadah is like a body without a soul. In addition to the danger on the left was the danger on the right. He would quote Hermann Cohen's quip that there are two kinds of rabbis: one who is willing to kill every *din* (law) for a Jew, and one who is willing to kill every Jew for a *din*. Believing both are wrong, Heschel did not hesitate to take up the claim of the latter as well as the former. Eloquent defender of tradition against the left, Heschel now becomes the critic of the extreme right.

He did so with notable credentials. Heschel had been a brilliant Talmud student. He studied with private tutors and then alone in the Bet Midrash, since it was not the custom of the Hasidim to send their sons away from the influences of home and family to attend yeshivot in distant towns. Among his teachers was the noted Rabbi Menahem Zemba of Warsaw. Heschel's first published writings at age fifteen were in one of the most respected halakhic journals in Warsaw.[26] Rabbi Hayim Zimmerman, the eminent talmudist, observed, after having read Heschel's work on rabbinic theology, *Torah min Hashamayin*, that it must have taken at least ten years of unremitting labor to write it. (Actually Heschel composed that work in two years, while involved in a number of other major projects, and without assistance. He later explained to me that, once he began, it just poured out as if it had been stored away in preparation for that moment.) At a family gathering at the time of his marriage, one rabbinic relative after another expounded his virtues, until the slight figure of his uncle, the Novominsker Rabbi, probably the most learned of all the Hasidic rabbis who had come to America, arose and objected: "Why are you praising him for all these gifts, which he certainly possesses? He is a great *lamdan* [talmudic scholar], a great *talmid hakham*, and that is more important than anything else."

Heschel understood that so legal a religion as Judaism faced "a perpetual danger of our observance and worship becoming mere habit."[27] He noted that in the seventeenth century Rabbi Isaiah Horowitz had observed that Jewish piety expressed itself over the centuries by continually adding to the requirements of the tradition. So fervent was spiritual intensity among Jews of the past, explained Heschel, that it was possible to expand the prayerbook, appending prayer upon prayer, and still pray with *kavana* or devotion. Now, however, we are faced with a dilemma in which we have kept the long prayers but no longer possess the inner spirit. "[O]bservance has, at times, become encrusted with so many customs and conventions that the jewel was lost in the setting." The tragedy was that "Outward compliance with externalities of the law took the place of the engagement of the whole person to the living God."[28] Some twenty-five hundred years ago Isaiah warned against mitzvot performed by rote *mitzvot melumadot*. To contend with this perennial problem, numerous attempts to renew Judaism have been made since the time of the Bible, most notably in recent times by Hasidism, which breathed new life into the law. However, as the time-span increased between themselves and the period of its founder, the Baal Shem (1690–1760), most Hasidim have become legalists as uncompromising as the others. In a greater or lesser measure, the modern movements of Haskala, Bundism, Zionism, and Reform were all directed against the uncompromising rigidity of nineteenth-century East European Judaism.

Ish Halakha

When J. B. Soloveitchik's essay *Halakhic Man* (*Ish Ha-halak-hah*) appeared, it was made the subject for a seminar session with Heschel. After each of us had our say, Heschel spoke. Most of his thoughts were later refined in print in various publications, but the freshness of the spoken word has its own merit. Here are his comments as I recorded them:

"*Ish Ha-halakha* [Halakhic Man]? *lo hayah velo nivra ela mashal hayah* [There never was such a Jew]! Soloveitchik's study, though brilliant, is based on the false notion that Judaism is a cold, logical affair with no room for piety. After all the Torah *does* say, 'Love the Lord thy God with all thy heart and soul and might.' No, there never was such a typology in Judaism as the halakhic man. There was—and is—an *Ish Torah* [a Torah man] who combines halakha and aggadah, but that is another matter altogether. When I came to Berlin, I was shocked to hear my fellow students talking about the problem of halakha as a central issue. In Poland it had been a foreign expression to me. Halakha is not an all-inclusive term, and to use it as such is to restrict Judaism. 'Torah' is the more comprehensive word. But the Orthodox often speak of halakha, instead of Torah. Halakha has very little to do with theology; in fact, some of them think that we have no need for theology at all. In the words of one Orthodox figure, '*shor shenagah es haporoh* is our theology.' (That is to say, the study of the Talmud, even such dry, legal portions as this—'assessing the damages done by an ox that gored a cow'—is all the theology needed.)[29]

"We are living in one of the periods of Jewish history when aggada has been devalued. For when you say ha-lakha, you exclude aggada. But they are inseparable. The Maharsha (R. Samuel Edels, d. 1631), whose greatness has not been sufficiently appreciated, composed two separate Talmud commentaries, one to the aggadah and one to the halakha. But, after completing them, in the introduction to the former he confesses to having erred, 'for one must not separate but join them as two sisters . . . for the halakhot and aggadot comprise one Torah for us' In such a person as the *Ish Ha-halakhah* [Halakhic man] there is little room for the spontaneous, for *rahamanut* [compassion]. The Jews in Alexandria mistakenly translated the Torah as *nomos*, law. But the [Aramaic] Targum translates it *orayta* or *rahmanut*. True, without halakha there can be no Judaism, but is halakha everything? Halakha is *din Torah* [the letter of the Law]. According to the Talmud, Jerusalem was destroyed because they were judging only according to *din Torah*, the letter of the Law, and not *lifnim mishurat hadin*, beyond the letter of the Law. The Law is necessary but not sufficient. 'Thou shalt be holy,' we are commanded. But what are the boundaries of holiness? Nahmanides reminds us that it is what God expects of us in *all* of life, both in that part which the Law covers and in that part which it does not, for 'it is possible to be a *naval* or scoundrel even while observing the Law.' What biblical passage is there, asks a Rabbinic sage, upon which all the Torah depends [*kol gufei Torah t'luiyim bo*]? He answers with the verse from Proverbs 3:6—'Serve Him in all your ways' [*B'khol d'rakhekha da-ei-hu*], that is to say, not only the prescribed legal ways but also in the ways for which there is no Law. It is this perspective which is being forgotten among those who exclusively stress halakha. Is not the verse, 'I have set the Lord before me at all times'—*Shiviti Adonoi l'negdi tamid*—at least as important as the passage, *Shor shenagah es haporoh*?

"The legalistic attitude has profoundly influenced Jewish observance, distorting ritual prescriptions over moral ones. Some Jews who refuse to discuss Torah [*dvar Torah*] without wearing a hat have no hesitation in repeating gossip [*lashon hara*] even while wearing a hat. Some who are upset by the bloodspot on an egg [which renders it un-kosher] ignore the bloodspot on a dollar bill. Why only *hashgaha* [religious supervision as to the proper observance of the Law] in restaurants but not in our banks, in butcher shops but not in our offices? We are alert to the laws of milk and meat but lax to the laws against lying and taking revenge [*Lo titor*; *midvar sheker tirhak* (Lev. 19:18; Ex. 23:7)]. Those halakhot have become 'mere' aggadot,[30] which is to say, they are not taken seriously. Now, what would happen if we were to turn some of the aggadot into halakhot? For example, despite the fact that the Talmud does not say, 'Cast yourself into the furnace rather than eat pork,' we are careful not to eat pork. But it does say 'Cast yourself into a furnace rather than shame another in public,' and still we ignore it. Perhaps changing such an aggada into halakha is the way to bring the Messiah?

"Halakha alone is not enough. The Law guides, but it needs the heart to guide also. Halakha is an *answer* to a question, namely: What does God ask of me? The moment that question dies in the heart, the answer becomes meaningless. That question, however, is agadic, spontaneous, personal. . . . The task of religious teaching is to be a midwife and bring about the birth of the question."[31]

Heschel continued his remarks on Soloveitchik by citing the Talmud: " 'Since the Temple was destroyed, all that has been left to the Lord is the four cubits of the halakha.'[32] This passage, usually understood in praise of the halakha, is nothing of the sort. It reflects not jubilation but remorse, as if to say: *Nebekh* [Alas], it was *takke shlekht* [unfortunate] that *Hakadosh Barukh Hu* [the Lord] was left with only the halakha!"

Elsewhere Heschel has written that in the exile "man's attentiveness to God became restricted to matters of halakha,"[33] as if He were absent from the wider world. But "A Judaism confined to the limits of the Halacha, with all due respect be it said, is not exactly one of the happiest products of the Diaspora."[34]

"One arch rabbinic expression of anti-aggadic bias questions the very order of events in the Torah. For if we take Torah to mean *nomos* or 'Law,' and understand it as the law book of Israel, then should it not have begun with the first law cited in it about the New Moon, which does not appear until the twelfth chapter of the Book of Exodus, and skip such less important, non-legal, aggadic chapters as creation, Adam and Eve, the flood, the lives of the patriarchs, and the

enslavement in Egypt!? That famous hasidic rabbi, Rashi"—
Heschel went on with a smile—"chooses to open his commentary to the Bible with a rejection of this very query.
Listen to how my ancestor, Rabbi Levi Yitzhak of Berditchev, dealt with the issue by paraphrasing Rashi's question—
Mah taam patah bivreishit ['What is the reason the Torah
begins with the story of creation and not the laws?']—into
the Yiddish, '*Vos far a "seese tam" pasah bivrayshis*—With
what a sweet taste did the Torah begin with the wonderful
stories of creation' [instead of with the laws of the new
moon, etc.]. 'The Torah,' added Heschel, 'is quite correct
to commence with the creation story rather than the legal
portions, for only a life-giver can be a law-giver.' "[35]

More than Halakha

Against those who argue that aggada is inauthentic, too individual and ephemeral, and that halakha is the only legitimate
guide to Jewish teaching, that Judaism is, as one scholar put
it, "halakhocentric," Heschel would contend that although
it may appear as if aggada has been subservient to halakha,
actually the reverse is the case: "halakha is dependent upon
aggada."[36] It provides the motivation, the vision, and the
values, for which halakha is the means, the expression, the
program. We understand halakha better than aggada because
of the excellent tradition, both oral and written, on the
meaning of the halakha. Aggada suffers from the lack of such
a continuous tradition. Even the scholars of the emancipation minimized the aggada, while the yeshivot would often
skip the aggada to get to the halakha. "Perhaps," Heschel
once suggested to me, "that is one of the reasons we are
having such problems with the halakha today—*because* we
skipped the aggada!" For Heschel believed that aggada, not
halakha, is the central problem today, and that once we clar-
ify ideological issues, then halakhic questions would more
easily fall into place.

In his monumental three-volume work, *Torah min Hashamayim: The Theology of Ancient Judaism*, Heschel demon-

strated the validity of his theory on the centrality of the aggada. "In order to appreciate what Heschel has achieved in this work," writes Jacob Neusner,

> one must keep in mind that until now we have had no really adequate explanation of the thought . . . behind the numerous sayings of talmudic rabbis dealing with matters of faith. . . . Heschel assumed . . . that certain figures should be made the focus of a historical-theological study, to see whether in a tentative fashion we may come to an adequate principle underlying and unifying their sayings and disputes. . . . Through an exhaustive examination of [Rabbi Akiba's and Rabbi Ishmael's] teachings, Heschel finds immanental opposed to transcendental religion, mysticism to rationalism. . . . Some have argued that aggadah, meaning religion and theology, . . . is irrelevant to Judaism. Judaism has no dogma, only halakhah—a law, a pattern of action. However, Jews are not robots, contented with mindless repetition of meaningless action. They have always . . . been thoughtful people. . . . Hence the aggadic parts of the Talmud . . . have been included in our tradition, not because ancient academicians could not find a better entertainment for their idle hours, as some exceptionally dull-souled expositors have maintained. Heschel has demonstrated in these volumes that the Rabbis were just as serious, just as penetrating, and just as self-consistent in theology as in law, for precisely the same reason, and in much the same manner. . . . And he has shown this not by preaching or arguing, but by a close and careful study of sources. Until now, we have had to accept the judgment that the Rabbis were not really interested in ideas, only in law. We no longer need to take seriously such a shallow opinion, for we can see it demonstrated with truly halakhic precision that the Rabbis of the Talmud were at least as concerned with theology as they were with law.[37]

Heschel called this common misunderstanding of Judaism "pan-halakhism," and the style of life that followed from it "religious behaviorism." Religious behaviorists usually "speak of discipline, tradition, observance, but never of religious experience, of religious ideas." For them, Judaism consists of "laws, deeds, things." Belief is not important, only keeping the law. Judaism, in this sense, becomes a kind of "sacred physics." Surprisingly, Heschel traces this notion to Spinoza, who argued that the Bible is not religion: it has " 'only very primitive notions' " of God. " 'Israelites knew scarcely anything of God,' " only law and politics—and to Mendelssohn, who claimed that " 'Judaism is no revealed religion . . . but only *revealed legislation* . . . freedom in doctrine and conformity in action.' " (It was from Spinoza, notes Heschel, that Kant and Hegel inherited the notion of the inferiority of the Bible.) According to Heschel, then, the two leading philosophers who prepared Jewry to enter into the new world of the West—and often out of Judaism altogether—paradoxically paved the way for the "Pan-Halachism" of the Orthodox.[38]

But Judaism is more than Law. "Halacha must not be observed for its own sake but for the sake of God. The law must not be idolized. It is a part, not all, of the Torah. We live and die for the sake of God rather than for the sake of the law."[39] Indeed, it is even possible to forget God in the punctilious observance of the Law.

> Judaism is not another word for legalism. The rules of observance are law in form and love in substance. The Torah contains both law and love. Law is what holds the world together; love is what brings the world forward. The law is the means, not the end; the way, not the goal. One of the goals is "Ye shalt be holy." The Torah is guidance to an end through a law. It is both a vision and a law. Man created in the likeness of God is called upon to re-create the world in the likeness of the vision of God. Halacha is neither the ultimate nor the all-embracing term for Jewish learning and living. . . . The Torah comprises both halacha and agada. Like body and soul, they are mutually dependent, and each is a dimension of its own.[40]

Furthermore, argued Heschel, built into Rabbinic law was a marvelous resiliency, a wonderful capacity for adapting to changing conditions and times, a capacity that has all but been stifled in certain circles. If some in the Reform camp think that they do not need the law, Heschel said, others in the Orthodox camp believe that they already possess it, holding that the law is unchangeable, fixed and final, once for all. This violates not only the canons of historical development but the very self-understanding of the Torah itself. The Law is anything but final. *"Judaism,"* writes Heschel, *"is based upon a minimum of revelation and a maximum of interpretation. . . . The Bible is a seed, God is the sun, but we are the soil."*

We are the soil! "Every generation is expected to bring forth new understanding and new realization." The authority to interpret is given to the sages, who "have the power to set aside a precept of the Torah when conditions require it. Here on earth, their opinion may [even] overrule an opinion held in heaven." The notion of the fluidity of the Law was carried to its extreme by Rabbi Menahem Mendl of Kotzk who expressed astonishment at the audacity of writing down the oral teaching during the time of the Talmud. So strict was the prohibition that doing so was likened to "burning the Torah." The Rabbis, nevertheless, felt "it is better that one part of the Torah shall be abrogated than [that] the whole Torah be forgotten. The accumulation of the vast amount of learning, the scattering of Jewish communities, and the weakening of memory militated against the oral system." They found authorization for their decision by reading Psalms 119:126 as: "There comes a time when you may abrogate the Torah in order to do the work of the Lord." How, the Kotzker asked, can one justify contravening what Jews, in obedience to clear prohibitions, refused to do for centuries? "The truth is," he explained, "that the oral law never has been written down. The meaning of the Torah," concludes Heschel, "has never been contained by books."[41]

Heschel was too awesome a person for me to challenge very often. One night, however, we had a discussion in his office that lasted several hours. The first volume of his *Torah min Hashamayim—A Theology of Ancient Judaism* had just been published. "Now that you have refuted the fixed notion of the tradition which has dominated so much of our thinking," I implored, "are you not obligated to take up the practical consequences? Must you not now demonstrate in the second volume how this understanding relates to the burning issues of revelation and halakha which so trouble us?" We talked until the early hours of the morning. It was then that he told me a story that illumined all that he had written about the Law and all that he had lived. It helped me to understand where he stood in the matter of Jewish observance.

"Sam," he said, "I am going to tell you a story I cannot tell anyone else here at the Seminary, because they [Lieberman? Finkelstein? both esteemed talmudists of the Lithuanian school] would not understand me. My father died when I was nine. At about fourteen or fifteen, I began to study Polish as a window to the wider world. We had no money for lessons, so my family in Vienna provided help. When they could no longer continue, I grew despondent. One Friday afternoon before services I was sitting on my father's chair in our *shtibl* [the Hasidic prayer house] in a sad mood. Itchi Meir Levin, a Kotzker Hasid who usually prayed with us on Shabbos, walked in. He was very close to me, a kind of mentor. I went over to him to discuss my problem, but he dismissed me with the words '*Di Gehenom brennt in mir.*' ['Hellfire burns in me.' That is, he was struggling to purify himself for the oncoming Sabbath, when the gates of hell were said to close, by ridding himself of the traces of Gehenom.] I returned to my chair and prayed the evening service with the small group of Hasidim who had arrived. Afterwards Itchi Meir, who observed my dismay, told me that the next morning before Sabbath services he would bring me a newly published booklet of the writings by my ancestor Pinhas of Koretz, the friend of the Baal Shem Tov.

"The next morning I was sitting alone in my father's seat before the quorum for prayer had gathered. Itchi Meir arrived and gave me the book he had promised. Eager to examine it, I took it and opened it. To my astonishment I discovered that it contained money, which, of course, is forbidden to be handled on the Sabbath. As if holding fire, I dropped the book immediately. But Itchi Meir calmed me down by explaining that according to Kotzk there are times when one may violate a minor law in order to perform a major mitzvah. He had known how important my Polish lessons were to me and had seen the despair on my face the previous evening on having to discontinue them. For a Hasid no sin is more grievous than despair. '*Atvsvus* [despair] on Shabbos!?' To save me from sadness he had violated the proscription against handling money on the Sabbath![42]

"Hasidism saved me for Judaism."

God, Israel, and Torah

In a little-known address given in Israel in 1972, shortly before his death, Heschel argued that the secret of Jewish survival is found in the famous statement: "God, Torah, and Israel are one." Or, more correctly, it is found in the proper balance among these three entities. He meant that as long as they were kept in balance through an harmonious relationship, one with the other, Jewish life would flourish despite the danger of outward conditions. But when they were in discord, when one of the three was stressed over another, or one neglected for the sake of another, then calamity threatened.

The three denominations of Judaism can be viewed from this vantage point. Reform, in an effort to clear away the overgrowth of custom and Law, and to rectify the chaotic reality of traditional Judaism, fell victim to its own revision by emphasizing theology to the neglect of Torah and the people-Israel. In the search for a "platform," whether the one that emerged from Pittsburgh in the nineteenth century or the one approved in Columbus in the twentieth, it lost the ground upon which to secure its goals. This neglect expressed itself (*a*) in its adoption of the Protestant Sunday School, despite the inadequacy of such a flimsy institution to transmit the highly intellectual and complicated tradition of Israel, to say nothing of the Hebrew language; (*b*) in a liturgy pruned of cantor, Hebrew, and passion; and (*c*) in its antinationalist and later anti-Zionistic position—"Berlin is our Jerusalem."

Imbalance similarly reveals the weakness of Conservatism in its stress on peoplehood—Clal Yisrael, Zionism, "Catholic Israel"—to the neglect of theology. This neglect is evident in its recent positions on abortion and homosexuality, which appear to be influenced more by the mood of the time than by the teachings of Judaism. Indeed, some conservatives have boasted of the absence of a unifying theology as a virtue of the movement.

Using his principle of harmony of God, Torah, and Israel, Heschel, in his last address in Israel in 1972, took up the question of the hardening of Orthodoxy, which was already affecting the culture of the State and would continue to affect its politics as well, culminating in the tragic assassination of Prime Minister Rabin.

> The role of Torah which has developed among our people is one of the wonders of Jewish history and has no parallel among any other nation. The problem, however, is that many *lamdanim* [Talmud scholars] in our time are so drunk with the love of the Torah that they sometimes forget the love of the Creator and the love of the people. . . . Some extremists appear to prefer Torah to God. Yes, we are commanded to love Torah, but we are also told to love God. Today there are those whose love of Torah threatens to supplant their love of God. And the love of God means love of His creatures, even those who have strayed from the path of Torah, and surely cannot mean, Heaven forbid, hatred of one's fellow-Jews, not uncommon today. Alas, the spirit of Satmar [Rabbi Joel Teitelbaum, d.1979, known for his narrow zealotry] hovers over our rabbis, while Reb Levi Yitzhak of Berditchev [known for his love for all Israel] has been forgotten. The demand of the hour is renewal, purification, vitality, but the extremist establishment stands like a medieval castle. Their leaders are busy erecting new fences and walls, instead of building a house for people to live in. As a result, Judaism looks like a jail to the young, instead of a fountain of life and joy. . . .[43]

There is a tradition that the Besht declared, "I came to teach love of God, love of Israel, and love of Torah." Con-

sistent with Heschel's theory of harmony of the three principles, he suggested that the Besht consciously changed the
accepted order, from God, Torah, and Israel, to God, *Israel*,
and Torah, in order to stress primacy to the people over
Torah. In this way the Baal Shem meant to counter the dangerous imbalance of the time, in which Torah was exalted at
the expense of the degradation of the mass of simple Jews
who were unlearned in Torah. For had it not been written
that the Torah was created for the sake of Israel? "The test
of love is in how one relates not to saints and scholars but to
rascals," wrote Heschel. "The Baal Shem related lovingly to
sinners who were not arrogant and kept his distance from
scholars who were."[44]

Heschel anticipated the growing confrontation with the
right in pointing to the limits of halakha alone. It is both too
short and too shallow: too short horizontally, in that, without the perspective of aggada, halakha penetrates only a part
of life, *all* of which is to be sanctified; and too shallow vertically, in that, without the dimension of aggada, even what
halakha does penetrate is penetrated inadequately. Heschel
once asked a class of students, "Is gelatin kosher?" This gave
rise to a lively discussion that he permitted to proceed for
several minutes. Then he stopped the discussion, noting that
the vigor of their opinions reflected the seriousness with
which they took the issue. "Now, tell me," he asked again,
"is the hydrogen bomb kosher?"[45] *See pg 120-21!*

Finally, Heschel stressed two fundamental halakhic guide-
lines from the sources of Judaism that are critical to those
who defend the center. First, Jewish law is not a matter of
all or nothing. This rejects fanaticism. Second, only general
principles—*klalim*—were revealed to Moses. This rejects
fundamentalism.[46] "The surest way of misunderstanding revelation," he wrote, "is to take it literally. . . ."[47]

As with his criticism of the left, so in his treatment of the
right, Heschel has provided us with a powerful constellation
of ideas around which to carry forth the analysis. Those that
I have considered here were:

The limits of halakha alone; responsibilities beyond the
Law; morality and the Law; religious behaviorism; pan-halakhism; the mobility of the Law; the fallacy of fundamentalism; the danger of atomization; a theology of aggada; and
the polarity of halakha and aggada.

Polarity

Heschel saw two dangers to our understanding of the law:
atomization and *generalization*. By generalization he meant focusing upon abstract man—inwardness, subjectivity, faith,
feeling, totality, without considering the concrete situation.
By atomization he meant the reverse, focusing upon a single
act, without considering the whole person, making it possible, for example, to admire one who is kosher although he
is also a liar. Further, atomization meant separating the part
from the whole, reducing Judaism to a system of ceremonies,
forgetting that above all single acts stands the command to
be a kingdom of priests and a holy people. Heschel argued
against these two extremes not only for theoretical reasons—
being a Jew was more than an idea to him—but also because
of his concern that at this moment in Jewish history when
the people-Israel, tottering and enfeebled from irreparable
losses, might easily lose their footing on the solid ground of
normative Judaism and topple into the pit of one side or the
other. Precisely this happened in the dark ages of the past.
Our situation, then, demands a reaffirmation of the center, a
center he sometimes described as "the tension of polarity."
A "*polarity*," he wrote,

> lies at the very heart of Judaism, the polarity of ideas and
> events, of mitsvah and sin, of kavanah and deed, of regularity
> and spontaneity, of uniformity and individuality, of halacha
> and agada, of law and inwardness, of love and fear, of under-
> standing and obedience, of joy and discipline, of the good and
> the evil drive, of time and eternity, of this world and the
> world to come, of revelation and response, of insight and in-
> formation, of empathy and self-expression, of creed and faith,
> of the word and that which is beyond words, of man's quest

for God and God in search of man. . . . There is no halacha without agada, and no agada without halacha. We must neither disparage the body, nor sacrifice the spirit. The body is the discipline, the pattern, the law; the spirit is inner devotion, spontaneity, freedom. The body without the spirit is a corpse; the spirit without the body is a ghost. Thus a mitsvah is both a discipline and an inspiration, an act of obedience and an experience of joy, a yoke and a prerogative. Our task is to learn how to maintain a harmony between the demands of halacha and the spirit of agada."[48]

Heschel's thought is a compelling argument for the vital center of Judaism. Mastering the broad range of Jewish thought and literature, he strove to restructure those parts of Judaism that, over the centuries, had taken on gruesome shapes. To use another metaphor: he sought to silence the cacophony of clashing sounds, the eerie clatter, the banging and clanging that the modern remnant of Israel had tragically come to express. He sought to repair the damaged instruments of Judaism, to find a new pitch to which all might be tuned. He strove to allow all the agents of Jewish thought and life to play harmoniously and melodiously under the direction of the Master, in contrast to those companies whose music is shrill, where lines are drawn and knives sharpened.

Conservative Judaism

Within the spectrum of denominations and institutions in modern Judaism, the Conservative movement and the Jewish Theological Seminary have always seen themselves as the Vital Center. Early leaders of the movement, such as Zechariah Frankel and Solomon Schechter, strove to ground that center, ideologically and academically, in the conviction that it represented the most authentic interpretation of Judaism and could best transmit the legacy of the past to the new Jewish world of the emancipated West. They sought to incorporate both the "left's" insights into modern thought and research, and the "right's" loyalty to the tradition, while at the same time refusing to succumb to the embrace of the homogeneous modernity of the one or the rigid fundamentalism of the other.

In the 1930s the eminent historian Salo Baron concluded his first, and some believe his finest, survey of Jewish history by focusing on the contemporary scene. After presenting a critical estimate of Reform, he argued that the Neo-Orthodoxy of Samson Raphael Hirsch, although claiming to save Judaism from the devastation of the reformers, in reality had much in common with them. For Neo-Orthodoxy, Baron argued, "accepted the premise of Reform that Judaism can be viewed as a dogmatic religion. Without being aware of it, Neo-Orthodoxy constituted in itself an equally fundamental deviation from historical Judaism. . . . No less than Reform, it abandoned Judaism's self-rejuvenating historical dynamism." Turning to the third alternative, Baron concluded that "the 'positive historical' Judaism of Zechariah Frankel and Michael Sachs, and the 'Conservative' Judaism of America, have been much truer to the spirit of traditional Judaism."[49]

However, what was true for the formative period of the movement, say from 1880 to 1920, was less so in the later years. Indeed, if viewed over the past half-century, it might appear that what Conservative Judaism negates has been clearer than what it affirms. This is the case, I suggest, because the process of formulating a philosophy for Conservative Judaism has been hampered by what, in time, came to be known as "Unity in Diversity."[50] While proposing to strengthen the movement by embracing all the various points of view, it became apparent that, with the exit of both the left-wing Reconstructionists and the right-wing Traditionalists into full-blown movements of their own, including rabbinical schools, congregational bodies, etc., that "unity in diversity" failed to achieve even this.[51] What it did achieve, however, was to halt that creative ideological process which had proved so fruitful in the movements's formative years and so promising for its future, and to turn Conservative Judaism into an amorphous umbrella under which even the most disparate views could find shelter. Thus the critical examination of texts and the exploration of the history of ideas or the philosophies (plural) of religion substituted for a systematic theology.[52]

The consequences have been unfortunate. For without such an ideology, Conservative Judaism has suffered a precarious anomalousness. The effect of "unity in diversity" has been to weaken Conservative Judaism's ability to fulfill the central role for which it was first established. Lacking clear parameters, the movement has, of late, been swept by the winds of gender and myth and threatened by the storm of political correctness.[53] Some yearn for a return to the time when devotion to the text was uppermost and theology was left to the individual student. In this time of historical upheaval when the virtue of moderation has fallen into disfavor, and extremism is on the rise among Jews as well as others, the role of the vital center takes on critical importance.

For those who wish to take up the task once again, Rabbi Abraham Joshua Heschel should be seen as the seminal figure for developing an ideology of the vital center of Judaism. Heschel's academic mastery of the diverse elements within Judaism and general culture, as well as his exposure to the piety and learning of Eastern Europe, the philosophy and method of Western Europe, and the democratic social concern of America, prepared him to become an interdisciplinary scholar who could view Judaism from the broadest perspective. Central to his approach and a key concept that runs through his writings is "polarity," or, better, the "tension of polarity." It is this approach as it applies to Jewish Law that he used to defend the centrist position against both the left and the right.

NOTES

1. A letter of December 27, 1972, from Rabbi Selig Auerbach to the Seminary chancellor on the death of Heschel reads: "I be-

lieve I have known Rabbi Heschel—zekher zaddik livrakha—
longer and perhaps even better than most people at our Seminary.
I met him first in Berlin when I was still a student at the Hildes-
heimer Rabbinerseminar, almost immediately when he came to
Berlin. He had already [received] semikha [ordination]. . . . He
gathered many students around him, mainly from the Rabbinerseminar [orthodox] and the Hochschule [liberal], and we knew we
could come to him with our problems at all hours of the day and
night. The Shabbat afternoons at his apartment corner Oranien-
burger and Artillerie Strasse will remain unforgettable to me. . . .
Although his way, for reasons unknown to me, led him to the
Hochschule, he always remained on most friendly terms with the
faculty and students of our Rabbinerseminar. My late teacher, Dr.
Wohlgemuth, always spoke very highly of Dr. Heschel . . ."
(Heschel Archives, JTS).

In his choice of schools, perhaps Heschel felt that the Orthodox
seminary had little to teach him, while he could explore Bible
criticism and modern Jewish thought more freely at the Liberal
school, where he remained fully observant.

2. God in Search of Man, p. 342.
3. Man's Quest for God, pp. 94–96, 99.
4. Ibid., p. 100, quoting p. 270 of Man Is Not Alone.
5. Notes of classes and personal discussions.
6. Man's Quest for God, p. 109.
7. Ibid., pp. 110–11, 110.
8. Ibid., p. 111.
9. Ibid., p. 106.
10. In the question-and-answer period after Heschel's address
to the HUC students we find his discussion of biblical categories
of thought.

"QUESTION: You mentioned the categories that form the Bible
which we have missed, because we have interpreted the Bible in
the light of other intellectual traditions. What are some of these
categories?

"ANSWER: I have tried to develop that idea in a small book . . .
about the Sabbath in which I tried to prove that biblical thinking
is time-oriented rather than space-oriented. Or in a study about
the prophets . . . I developed a number of ideas that are at home
in the Bible but not at home, let us say, in Greek thinking.

"The problem of anthropomorphism arose in a misunderstanding of biblical thinking. To the Bible the idea of God having a

pathos, that is, God standing in an emotional relationship to the world, is profoundly significant, because it presupposes a different metaphysics, from, let us say, the metaphysics of Parmenides. Consequently, later, in the encounter of Greek philosophy with the Bible, a tension arose. There are different presuppositions. For example, the presence of God in the world. Plato's philosophy begins without God. Since that time philosophy of religion begins exactly like Plato, with the givenness of the world but with the non-givenness of God. That is the classic position. Now, it is quite different in the Bible. In biblical tradition it is inconceivable to think of the world without believing in God. It is just inconceivable. Western man has been trained in a way of thinking that takes this world for granted, as a matter of fact—as a matter of *fact*; and we are not amazed, nor do we wonder at it. And then we try to bring in God. That is a very difficult matter. It is the other way around in the Bible.

"The Bible gives me many categories. The categories developed in my book *Man Is Not Alone* are taken from biblical thinking, and in a forthcoming book [*God in Search of Man*] I will show that these ideas are a manifestation of biblical categories. For example, the problem of amazement in regard to nature. Biblical man says, the heaven declares the glory of God. The Greek mind does not understand this. In the mythology of other nations, while it is quite conceivable that God should become a star, that the star should sing to God would be an absurdity. But in the Bible that star sings to God. The whole of nature utters praise to God. How strange! Was the biblical man mad? Or perhaps he sensed something that we cannot sense because we are using different categories" (Unpublished address to HUC students in Cincinnati, after CCAR address; tape in American Jewish Archives).

    11. Michael Satlow, "Jewish Knowing: Monism and Its Ramifications," *Judaism*, 45 (1996), 483–89.
    12. *God in Search of Man*, p. 343.
    13. Ibid., pp. 343, 344–45.
    14. *Man's Quest for God*, p. 112.
    15. *The Earth Is the Lord's*, pp. 61–63.
    16. See Dresner, *The Zaddik*.
    17. Fortunately, the session was recorded.
    18. Note the distinction made between halakha and halakhiyut. While one may change or neglect this or that law, the principle of Jewish Law must not be abandoned.

19. The first two letters of the Hebrew word for Jew, *Yehudi*, form YH, part of YHVH, the ineffable name of God. Heschel's book of poetry was named *Der Shem Hameforash: Mentsh* (Man: The Ineffable Name of God).

20. Martin I. Lockshin, "Orthodox 'Intolerance': A Blessing?" *Sh'ma*, November 14, 1986.

21. Another factor in the rise of the extremism of the right may be the fact that it was Hungarian rather than Polish and Lithuanian Jewry who survived.

22. TB Hagigah 15a.

23. See Alan Yuter, "Positivist Rhetoric and Its Functions in Haredi Orthodoxy," *Jewish Political Studies Review*, 8 (1996), 127–88, and the literature quoted there.

24. For a review of the literature on whether Christians are to be considered idolaters, see the late nineteenth-century responsum of Rabbi Marcus Horovitz, the chief rabbi of Frankfurt, to the question, "Is it permissible for a Jew to contribute to the building of a church?" (*Mateh Levi* [Jerusalem: Jerusalem Academy Publications, 1979], Part 2, #28, pp. 80–85).

25. Yuter, "Positivist Rhetoric and Its Functions in Haredi Orthodoxy," 150.

A glaring example of how radical the change has been in the process of Orthodoxy's delegitimization of the Conservative Movement, now lumped together with Reform to form "Liberal Judaism," is the fact that when the important chair in Talmud became available in the 1930s with an eye on the eventual retirement of Rabbi Louis Ginzberg, the three most important candidates who applied were, according to Wolfe Kelman, J. B. Soloveitchik, Samuel Belkin, and Saul Lieberman.

26. "Hidushei Torah" in *Sha'arei Torah, kovetz hodshi* (Warsaw), 13, No. 1, (1922), "Bet Midrash," Part 1, no. 4, Sect. 78; ibid., no. 2 (1923), "Bet Midrash," part 1, No. 6, Sect. 108.

27. *God in Search of Man*, p. 343.

28. Ibid., p. 326.

29. Saul Lieberman, the renowned talmudist at the Jewish Theological Seminary, who typified this view, referred to "*pit-pat* (Hebrew for 'prattle' or 'babel') theology." In once introducing the leading authority on the history and meaning of Jewish mysticism, Gershom Scholem, who had been brought from Israel for a major lecture at the Seminary, Lieberman said the following: "Mysticism is nonsense. But the history of mysticism—that is another matter!"

30. The non-legal portions of the Talmud: narrative, exegesis, legend, or lore.

31. *God in Search of Man*, p. 339.

32. TB Berakhot 8a.

33. *God in Search of Man*, p. 331.

34. *The Insecurity of Freedom*, p. 198.

35. *God in Search of Man*, p. 328.

36. Ibid.

37. Jacob Neusner, review of Heschel's *Theology of Ancient Judaism*, *Conservative Judaism*, 20, No. 3 (1966), 67–69. For a different view from Heschel's, see "Thought as Reflected in the Halakhah" by Louis Ginzberg in his *Students, Scholars and Saints* (Philadelphia: Jewish Publication Society, 1928), esp. pp. 114–18. Ginzberg finds the "authoritative character" of Judaism in the halakha. The "Haggadah," he argues, consists of "opinions and views uttered by Jewish sages for the most part on the spur of the moment." To one who would attempt to create a theology from the aggada, Ginzberg would respond, "You are utterly wrong in your attempts to stamp as an expression of the Jewish soul what is only an individual opinion or a transitory fancy. It is only in the Halakhah that we find the mind and character of the Jewish people exactly and adequately expressed. . . . Religion is law for the Jews" (pp. 115–18).

38. *God in Search of Man*, pp. 320–22.

39. Ibid., p. 326.

40. Ibid., pp. 323–24.

41. Ibid., pp. 274 (emphasis added), 275, 276. TB Berakhot 54a. Levi Isaac ben Meir, *Kedushat Levi ha-halem* (Jerusalem: Ha-Mosad le-hotsa'at sifre musar va Hasidut, 1964), pp. 306–307, likutim.

42. For the sin of sadness in Hasidism, see Jacob Joseph of Polonnoye, *Ben Porat Yosef* (Koretz, 1781) 64a, and Samuel H. Dresner, "Hasidism and Its Opponents," in R. Jospe, *Great Schisms in Jewish History* (New York: Ktav, 1984), pp. 128–38, esp. note 8.

43. Abraham J. Heschel, "The Jewish People and the Zionist Movement" (Hebrew), World Zionist Congress, Jerusalem, 1972, pp. 55–60.

44. *A Passion for Truth*, pp. 65, 66.

45. In the following incident one can discern the subtle relationship Heschel felt between halakha and aggada. Jewish Law or halakha appears to respond to the demands of modernity in three ways: Orthodoxy, more or less, ignores it and maintains the ha-

lakha unchanged; Reform, more or less, succumbs to the challenge at the expense of the Law; Conservativism, struggling to preserve what they can, is torn in two directions. One of the most unwise decisions of their Committee on Law and Standards was, under certain circumstances, to permit riding to the synagogue on the Sabbath. I recall Heschel's sarcastic response.

"Don't think I don't appreciate the kind intentions of the members of the law committee," he told a few of us. "They want to make it easier for me to get to the synagogue on Shabbat. After all, it is quite a long walk, especially in bad weather, and they have pity on me. But, you know, I really don't mind the walk. It is good exercise, and usually there are others to walk and chat with. Furthermore, we are a small people and living within walking distance to the synagogue has always helped to maintain a Jewish community. So, I say to the law committee, thank you, but no thanks.

"However, if the law committee really wants to help me, I could make a suggestion to them. I have always been overwhelmed by the commandment 'You shall love the Lord your God with all your heart. . . .' That obligation is a terrible burden, an impossible responsibility. Now, if the law committee wants to ease that ordeal, let them emend that law to: 'You shall love the Lord your God with *half* your heart. . . .'"!

46. *God in Search of Man*, p. 302.

47. Ibid., p. 178.

48. Ibid., p. 341.

49. Salo Baron, *A Social and Religious History of the Jews* (New York: Columbia University Press, 1937), vol. 2, pp. 257–58.

50. M. M. Kaplan, "Unity in Diversity" (New York, United Synagogue of America, 1947). Cf. Samuel H. Dresner, "Rabbi," *Conservative Judaism*, 45, No. 2 (1993), 8–11.

51. A further sign of destabilization was the 1995 declaration of the University of Judaism, the former West Coast branch of the Jewish Theological Seminary, as an independent institution with its own rabbinical school. Although it still maintains ties with the mother institution, it is too early to determine to what extent the more liberal atmosphere of the West Coast will affect the new school. Though this break-off differs from the former two in being less a matter of philosophy than of funding, it nevertheless reflects the fragmentation of the movement.

52. Robert Gordis's *Conservative Judaism* (1945), Mordecai

Waxman's *Tradition and Change* (1949), and even *Emet Ve-Emunah: A Statement of Principles of Conservative Judaism* (1988) all suffer from an eclecticism and an historicism—so and so said such and such—that serve as a substitute from the stated goal of formulating "a statement of principles of Conservative Judaism." *Emet Ve-Emunah* is a case in point. While both the "Pittsburgh" and the "Columbus" platforms of the Reform Movement of the nineteenth and twentieth centuries were clear and concise statements of Reform Judaism, the pronouncement of the Conservatives is anything but. To guarantee inclusivity, no fewer than three cumbersome forewords, representing the academy, the congregational rabbis, and the laymen, followed by a formal introduction by the chairman, precede and overwhelm the statement itself. Further, the Seminary's own leading theologians, Fritz Rothschild and Seymour Siegel, were not members of the commission that drew up the document. (Though Siegel is listed, he did not serve.)

Instead of producing a clear, brief document of principles as Reform had done, this statement presents too often a diffuse collection of differing views. "For *many Conservative Jews*, Halakhah is indispensable. . . ." "It is what *the Jewish community* views God's will to be. . . ." "The divine element of Jewish law is understood *in various ways* within the Conservative community. . . ." "*Some*" (Conservative Jews) accept a literal view of revelation; "*others*" do not. "*Our ancestors believed* themselves chosen to be a kingdom of priests and a holy nation," but "even *those who do not* accept the belief in 'the chosen people' . . ." Further, we are told of "revolutionary messianists," and "messianic gradualists"; and that "*for many of us*, belief in God means . . ." but that, on the other hand, "*some* view the reality of God differently" (emphasis added). Readers, however, are less interested in what Conservative "Jews" believe than in what Conservative "Judaism" teaches. They know that Conservative Jews hold a variety of beliefs, as indeed do Orthodox and Reform Jews. What has not been made clear is what Conservative *Judaism* has to say about God, revelation, halakha and the chosen people. This is difficult to discern from this document, and leaves searching Conservative Jews in the same state of confusion they were in was before they examined this booklet of "principles." In short, the statement contains neither the clarity of Will Herberg nor the lyric profundity of Abraham Heschel, a terse summary of either or both would have served their purposes better.

53. The movement's most recent evidence of political correctness has been a new "gender-sensitive" prayer book, a revised rabbinic manual with a blessing for abortion, and a repudiation of Judaism's family-centered warnings against homosexuality.

BIBLIOGRAPHY

Adler, Elkan. *Jews in Many Lands*. Philadelphia: Jewish Publication Society, 1905.

Balaban, M. "Hasidut," *Hetekufa*, 18 (1923), 488.

Baron, Salo. *A Social and Religious History of the Jews*. Vol. 2. New York: Columbia University Press, 1937.

————. "Steinschneider's Contribution to Historiography." *Alexander Marx Jubilee Volume*. New York: Jewish Theological Seminary, 1950.

Biale, David. *Gershom Scholem*. Cambridge, Mass.: Harvard University Press, 1979.

Biderman, I. *Mayer Balaban: Historian of Polish Judaism*. New York: Biderman Book Committee, 1976.

Bromberg, A. *Hasidic Leaders* (Hebrew). Vol. 20. Jerusalem: Hamakhon Lehasidut, 1963.

Buber, Martin. *Briefwechsel aus sieben Jahrzehnten*. Ed. Grete Schaeder. Heidelberg: L. Schneider, 1972.

————. "Interpreting Hasidism," *Commentary*, 36, No. 3 (1963), 218–25.

————. *Jüdische Bewegung*. Vol. 1. Berlin: Jüdische Verlag, 1920.

————. "Jüdische Wissenschaft." *Die Welt*, 11–12 (October 1901).

————. "Replies to My Critics: On Hasidism." In *The Philosophy of Martin Buber*. Ed. Paul Schilpp and Maurice Friedman. La Salle, Ill.: Open Court, 1967. Pp. 731–41.

Cohen, Arthur. "Martin Buber and Judaism." *Leo Baeck Yearbook 25*. London: Secker & Warburg, 1980. Pp. 287–300.

"Contemporary Judaism and the Christian." *America*, 128 (March 10, 1973), p. 12.

Davies, W. D. "Conscience, Scholar, Witness." *America*, 128 (March 10, 1973), pp. 213–15.

Dresner, Samuel H. "Hasidism and Its Opponents." In Raphael Jospe. *Great Schisms in Jewish History.* New York: Ktav, 1984. Pp. 128–38.

————. "Is Bashevis Singer a Jewish Writer?" *Midstream*, 27, No. 3 (1980), 42–47.

————. "Rabbi." *Conservative Judaism*, 45, No. 2 (1993), 8–11.

————. *The Zaddik.* New York and London: Abelard-Schuman, 1960. Repr. New York: Schocken Books, 1974. Repr. New York: Aronson, 1994.

Elbogen, Ismar. *Der jüdische Gottesdienst in seiner geschichtlichen Entwicklung.* Leipzig: Fock, 1913. *Jewish Liturgy: A Comprehensive History.* Trans. Raymond Scheindlin. Philadelphia: Jewish Publication Society, 1993.

Eliach, Y. "The Russian Dissenting Sects and Their Influence on Israel Baal Shem Tov, Founder of Hasidism." *Proceedings of the American Academy for Jewish Research*, 36 (1968), 57–81.

Etkes, E. "The System of R. Hayim of Volozhin as a Response of the Community of the Mitnagdim to Hasidism" (Hebrew). *Proceedings of the American Academy for Jewish Research*, 39 (1972), 1–46 (Hebrew Section).

Fine, R. "Solomon Schechter and the Ambivalence of Jewish *Wissenschaft.*" *Judaism*, 46 (Winter 1997), 3–24.

Freiman, A. *Katalog der Judaica.* Frankfurt: Lehrberger, 1922.

Friedman, Maurice. *Martin Buber's Life and Work.* 3 vols. New York: E. P. Dutton: 1981–1983.

Gedalia of Linitz. *Teshu'ot Hen.* Jerusalem: S. Reigen, 1964.

Ginzberg, Louis. *Students, Scholars and Saints.* Philadelphia: Jewish Publication Society, 1928.

Glatzer, Nahum N. "Reflection on Buber's Impact on German Jewry." *Leo Baeck Yearbook 25.* London: Secker & Warburg, 1980. Pp. 301–309.

Golinkin, E., ed. *The Responsa of Professor Louis Ginzberg.* New York: Jewish Theological Seminary, 1996.

Graetz, Heinrich. *History of the Jews*. Vol. 5. Philadelphia: Jewish Publication Society, 1898.

Haam, Ahad (Asher Ginzberg). *Al Parashat Derakhim*. 2 vols. Berlin: Dvir, 1913.

Heschel, Abraham Joshua. *Between God and Man: From the Writings of Abraham J. Heschel*. Ed. Fritz A. Rothschild. New York: Harper & Brothers, 1959. Rev. repr. New York: Free Press, 1965.

———. *The Circle of the Baal Shem Tov: Studies in Hasidism*. Ed. Samuel H. Dresner. Chicago: The University of Chicago Press, 1985. Rev. ed. New York: Jewish Theological Seminary, 1998.

———. *The Earth Is the Lord's: The Inner World of the Jew in Eastern Europe*. New York: Henry Schuman, Inc., 1950.

———. *God in Search of Man: A Philosophy of Judaism*. New York: Farrar, Straus, & Cudahy, 1955.

———. "Hasidism." *Jewish Heritage*, 14, No. 3 (1972), 1–21.

———. "In Search of Exaltation." *Jewish Heritage*, 13 (Fall, 1971), 29–35.

———. *The Insecurity of Freedom*. New York: Schocken Books, 1966.

———. "The Jewish Notion of God and Christian Renewal." In *Renewal of Religious Thought*. Vol. 1 of *Theology of Renewal*. Ed. L. K. Shook. New York: Herder & Herder, 1968. Pp. 105–29.

———. "The Jewish People and the Zionist Movement" (Hebrew). World Zionist Congress, Jerusalem, 1972. Pp. 55–60.

———. *Kotzk: In Gerangel far Emesdikeit* (Kotzk: The Struggle for Integrity). 2 vols. Tel Aviv: Hamenora, 1973.

———. *Man Is Not Alone: A Philosophy of Religion*. New York: Farrar, Straus, and Young, 1951.

———. *Man's Quest for God: Studies in Prayer and Symbolism*. New York: Charles Scribner's Sons, 1954.

———. "No Religion Is an Island." *Union Seminary Quarterly Review*, 21 (January 1966), 117–34 (p. 119).

———. *A Passion for Truth*. New York: Farrar, Straus, &

Giroux, 1973. Repr. New York: Noonday, 1974; Woodstock, Vt.: Jewish Lights Publishing, 1995.

———. "The Two Great Traditions: The Sephardim and the Ashkenazim." *Commentary*, 5 (1948), 416–22.

———. "Reb Pinkhes Koretzer." *YIVO Bleter*, 33 (1949), 9–48.

———. "Unknown Documents in the History of Hasidism" (Yiddish). *YIVO Bleter*, 36 (1952), 113–35.

Jacobson, Gershon. Interview with Heschel. *Day-Morning Journal*, June 13, 1963.

Kaplan, Edward K., and Samuel H. Dresner. *Abraham Joshua Heschel*. New Haven, Conn.: Yale University Press, 1998.

Kaplan, Mordecai M. "Unity in Diversity." New York, United Synagogue of America, 1947.

Keter Shem Tov. Brooklyn: Kehot, 1972.

Levi Isaac ben Meir. *Kedushat Levi ha-shalem*. Jerusalem: Ha-Mosad le-hotsa'at sifre musar va Hasidut, 1964.

Lieberman, H. "How Jewish 'Researchers' Explore Hasidism" (Hebrew). *Ohel Rahel*. Vol. 1. Brooklyn: Empire Press, 1980. Pp. 1–49.

L'Yaakov, Devrav, ed. *Dov Ber, Maggid of Miedzyrzecz* (Mezeritch). Jerusalem: Hebrew University Press, 1976.

Marty, Martin. "A Giant Has Fallen." *The Christian Century*, 19 (January 17, 1973), 87.

Nash, Stanley. *In Search of Hebraism: Shai Hurwitz and His Polemics in the Hebrew Press*. Leiden: Brill, 1980.

———. "The Psychology of Dynamic Self-Negation in a Modern Writer, Shai Hurwitz (1861–1922)." *Proceedings of the American Academy for Jewish Research*, 44 (1977), 81–93.

Neusner, Jacob. Review of *Theology of Ancient Judaism* by Abraham Joshua Heschel. *Conservative Judaism*, 20, No. 3 (1966), 67–69.

Niebuhr, Reinhold. "Masterful Analysis of Faith." *New York Herald Tribune Book Review*, 118 (April 1, 1951), p. 12.

Piekarz, M. *Bimey Tzemihat Hahasidut*. Jerusalem: Mosad Bialik, 1978.

Rabinowicz, H. *The World of Hasidism*. London: Valentine, 1970.

Rosenzweig, Franz. "The Builders: Concerning the Law." In *On Jewish Learning.* Ed. Nahum N. Glatzer. New York: Schocken Books, 1955. Pp. 72–92.

Rosman, Murray Jay. *Founder of Hasidism: A Quest for the Historical Ba'al Shem Tov.* Berkeley: University of California Press, 1966.

Rothschild. Fritz A., ed. *Between God and Man: From the Writings of Abraham J. Heschel.* New York: Harper & Brothers, 1959. Rev. rept. New York: Free Press, 1965.

Satlow, Michael. "Jewish Knowing: Monism and Its Ramifications." *Judaism,* 45 (1996), 483–89.

Schatz, R. "Gershom Scholem's Interpretation of Hasidism as an Expression of His Philosophy of Idealism" (Hebrew). In *Gershom Scholem: The Man and His Work* (Hebrew). Jerusalem: Israel National Academy for Science/Magnes Press–Mosad Bialik, 1994. Pp. 48–63.

Schatz-Uffenheimer, Rivkah. "Man's Relation to God and the World in Buber's Rendering of the Hasidic Teaching." In *The Philosophy of Martin Buber.* Ed. Paul Schilpp and Maurice Friedman. La Salle, Ill.: Open Court, 1967. Pp. 403–35.

Schechter, Solomon. *The Chassidim.* London: Jewish Chronicle, 1887.

Schneirson, Fischel. "Ani Maamin" (I Believe). Trans. Samuel Dresner. *Conservative Judaism,* 22 (Spring 1968), 20–30.

Scholem, Gershom. *Devarim Bago.* Tel Aviv: Am Oved, 1975.

———. "Martin Buber's Conception of Judaism." *On Jews and Judaism in Crisis.* New York: Schocken Books, 1976. Pp. 126–72.

———. "M. Buber's Interpretation of Hasidism." In *The Messianic Idea in Judaism.* New York: Schocken Books, 1971. Pp. 227–51.

———. *Sabbatai Sevi: The Mystical Messiah, 1626–1676.* Princeton, N.J.: Princeton University Press, 1973.

Schulman, Elias. *Yung Vilne, 1929–1939* (Yiddish). New York: Getseltn, 1946.

Schweid, Eliezer. "Mysticism and Judaism According to Gershom Scholem" (Hebrew). *Jerusalem Studies in Jewish Thought*, Supplement 2 (1983).

Setzer, S. Biography of the Besht. *Bicher Velt*, 1, Nos. 4–5 (1922), 406–407.

Simon, Ernst A. "Martin Buber and the Faith of Israel" [Hebrew]. *Divre 'iyun mukdashim le-Mordekhai Martin Buber* (Contemplations dedicated to Mordecai Martin Buber on the occasion of his eightieth birthday). Jerusalem: Magnes, 1958. Pp. 13–56.

Singer, Isaac Bashevis. *A Young Man in Search of Love*. Garden City, N.Y.: Doubleday, 1978.

Twerski, A. *The Genealogy of Tchernobl and Ruzhin* (Hebrew). Lublin, 1938.

Weiss, J. "The Great Maggid's Theory of Contemplative Magic." *Hebrew Union College Annual*, 31 (1960), 137–48.

Wilensky, M. "Some Notes on Rabbi Israel Loebel's Polemic Against Hasidism." *Proceedings of the American Academy for Jewish Research*, 30 (1962), 141–51.

Yuter, Alan. "Positivist Rhetoric and Its Functions in Haredi Orthodoxy." *Jewish Political Studies Review*, 8 (1996), 127–88.

INDEX

May 2010, Aug. 2011, June 2013, Dec. 2014 —
March 2018, March '21,